Is Your Horse a Rock Star?

Rock Star?

Understanding Your Horse's Personality

Dessa Hockley

2008

Is Your Horse a Rock Star?

Contents

Acknowledgements

I would like to acknowledge and thank the following for helping make this book happen: Jane Smiley, author and creator of the idea that has consumed my life for the past 3 years; Marg Krastel and Cathy Thomas, my horsey friends, for all their time editing and talking about my project; Dave Elston for his creative horse personality illustrations; Rosie Williams, Andrea Harris, Nicole Mason, Angie Benson, Rise Massey, trainer friends who have helped develop the systems that all the different horses need; all my riding students who have tested this material on their horses; all the fabulous horses that I have known over the years; Denton Hockley, Megan MacDonald and Henry for their love and encouragement; and especially my best friend and partner, Larry Verhulst, who allowed me the luxury of the time to work on this project. I couldn't have done it without you all.

Introduction

Personality testing for horses: This is not a scientific study. No doctorates here. These are just the observations of a woman who has loved and worked with horses all her life and constantly questioned, "Why?" Why is this horse so much harder to handle than that one? Why, when I have twenty babies to halter break, are there two or three that do not respond to the same training program—and why do I find myself with one little rascal dallied around an evergreen tree and me yelling for some assistance? Why is it that the sweetest colt in the herd is the one that blows up and bucks you off? Why is it that the horse you have raised yourself, imprinted and handled every day is now ten years old and has you totally bamboozled? You still have to treat him like a two year-old, and you shake your head and wonder how you made a career with horses.

In the quest for understanding, I have subscribed to every horse philosophy: Ray Hunt, Pat Parelli, John Lyons, Chris Irwin, Monty Roberts, and so on. But I was still left with questions. Then along comes a nice read in the form of Jane Smiley's book, *A Year at the Races*, and in one small chapter in the middle of the book comes a big "WOW" for me. Horse Personality testing! I am driving across the Canadian prairies by myself and madly putting all the horses I have owned into their personalities when I realize that Saskatchewan has flown by. Now that does not usually happen. This is good. I get home and put all the horses I have taught over the years into their respective slots and some common denominators start to show up.

So that is why my "sweety" bucks me off. She is a Wall Flower (Submissive, Lazy, Afraid and Friendly). She is very, very sweet, but I pushed her when I needed to listen to her. And that is why my "10 year-old-slash-2 year-old" has fallen through the cracks. He's a DLAA (Dominant, Lazy, Afraid and Aloof). That does not spell easy as you will see when you read about the Skeptic! This horse needed to be handled differently. For one thing he needed a job and he is now ten years old and does not have one. Not all horses want to be the friendly pleasure horse even if we think that would be the ideal life.

So this is how personality testing works. Once we know what personality our horses are, then we can quit trying to stuff that round peg into the square hole.

The wheels are turning—what if we could personality test our foals? We would know immediately if they needed us to be there for them every step (Submissive) or needed us to turn them loose and let them figure things out (Dominant). Are they fearful and need the slow program, or are they curious and need a lot of variety? Do they need a job, or are they just happy to please us? So many questions and so many places I see my training program needing to change.

I teach some weekend riding workshops. Those horses should not all be doing the same exercises. Some are bored to tears and some are terrified. I feel like a lot of school teachers must. I find myself teaching to the middle segment, and the top and bottom horses are struggling. On the one end are the DECF's (the Rock Stars). They have the super egos, are super confident, super friendly—the all round guys. They thrive on challenge and change. They are not being challenged. On the other end you might find the SLAA's (the Lone Wolves). They do not like new places or to learn new things. These horses need their security blankets to leave home. Just being at a new barn with all the new horses around is almost more than they can bear. They need a quiet little corner and an exercise that is not too challenging. They want to do it well, and it needs to have purpose for them to feel safe. These two personalities need programs that are extremely different; I need to teach from a different perspective.

Perhaps by understanding your horse's personality a new and exciting world will open up for you as well. Can you see where the training program needs to change? Maybe the sport is all wrong for him and that is why the two of you have been struggling.

Perhaps dressage is boring for him and he needs to be a show jumper; maybe the show jumper is too afraid and stressed and needs to be the dressage horse; maybe your horse has too much energy to be an arena horse and needs to get out on the trail and pound away some miles; or maybe you will be able to combine the two like a friend of mine did with her wonderful little Arab mare named Sam. We had been working on teaching her to jump, and it was proving to be a difficult process. She was hot, would get quick, run off, and even buck on occasion. Her energy was being directed in the wrong place. Then one year, she became a pleasure to jump. She started to quietly "hunter" down lines. The reason for the big change? Her owner had begun training her in distance riding. Sam needed to go out and do a 25- to 50-mile ride a week to be able to settle down in her ring work. Sam is an SECF (Submissive, Energetic, Curious and Friendly). These letters say she needs a lot of variety. But what she mostly needed was her big E (Energetic) satisfied. We discovered this by accident. But now that we can test our horses and know what type they are, we can design a program that is perfect for them.

Another horse I taught carries the traits Curious and Aloof. Like Sam, this horse needed variety in his jobs. Louie is a Warmblood whose owner had been training him as a show jumper. She had heard about an animal communicator from California and thought it would be fun to hear what her horses had to say via the communicator. The first thing Louie said was: "I'd like to be a western horse." Now the whole family stood and stared with their mouths open in shock. After all the money and training and horse show fees they put into him, he wanted to be a western horse?!? They called me in disbelief and horror. At the time, I couldn't explain it by personality, saying, "Oh, he has a big C (Curious) so he needs lots of different things to do." But I did try to pacify them and say that I'm sure he just wants to try something different. He is very confident in his jumping—new fences only interest him for a couple of times. What harm would it do to put a different saddle on him and go ride in the mountains or teach him the barrels or go move neighbors' cows? His owner was game and let him play at a variety of new sports, and he loved it! His jumping only got better. By the fall indoor Spruce Meadows show he was happy to be there and very confident and competitive in the ring. Although her jumping coach did say, "You will have to watch those corners—you are starting to look like a barrel racer!"

Delve into it and see what personalities are out in your pasture. The descriptions under each of the eight characteristics or traits will help you decide which category your horse is in. Put the letters together and hopefully that knowledge will open a new door for you. It should help you avoid getting bucked off, run over, run away with, or stepped on (that's a favorite of the Afraid/Friendly).

Horse personalities apply to both genders. For example, a Goddess can be either male or female. You will notice that Dominant horses will seem male and Submissive horses will seem female, but they can be either. This could be the energy they exude, and I'll talk more about this as we go. For the purposes of this book, I will be using the masculine for all horses, recognizing that the personalities could be either male or female.

Throughout the book, I refer to some "Tools" or strategies for working with different types of horses. A brief description of each of these tools is at the end of the book. Specific riding or training "how to's" are readily available in books, workshops and videos and so are not included here. I challenge you to use your creativity when developing your program. Get some basic instruction, but do not be afraid to use your own horse communication skills to listen and see what works for you and your horse.

So my journey into understanding horses is expanding even as I am writing this book. I continue to test horses—the number is over 500 now and growing. The more you come to accept them for who they are and listen to what they need, the more they will honor you and accept your requests. This is definitely what I have found. May this information help you to enjoy your horse more and to see his funny idiosyncrasies and oddities as personality-related, not something that needs to be fixed.

The Eight Personality Traits

Dominant or Submissive: How much control do they need in their world?

Energetic or Lazy: How much effort do they put in? How do they express themselves? How much energy do they carry?

Curious or Afraid: How do they approach life and learning?

Friendly or Aloof: How are they motivated? How do they fit in socially?

By combining the above eight traits, sixteen different personalities emerge. Personality testing for people has been used for years to help people in the work place and in personal relationships to better understand each other: how they fit in socially, how they view their world, how they need to spend their time, what fills them up, and what motivates them. By answering some questions we come to understand our preferences for how and why we do things. Ideally, this helps us learn to accept ourselves and become what we were meant to be. The same can hold true for horses. Each horse is born with a unique personality. The more we understand it, the more we can customize our program and allow the true spirit of that unique horse to emerge.

The Sixteen Personality Types
The Dominants

DECF	The Rock Star
DECA	The Macho Man
DEAF	The Wild Card
DEAA	The Boss
DLCF	The Reluctant Rock Star
DLCA	The Prize Fighter
DLAF	The Accountant
DLAA	The Skeptic

The Submissives

SECF	The Goddess
SECA	The Worker Bee
SEAF	The People Pleaser
SEAA	The Perfectionist
SLCF	The Steady Eddy
SLCA	The Solo Artist
SLAF	The Wall Flower
SLAA	The Lone Wolf

Section I

The Eight Personality Traits

Chapter 1

Dominant or Submissive

Where does your horse fit in? In the herd, which horses are more dominant than yours, which are more submissive? The more dominant the horse, the higher up he will be in the pecking order and the more control he needs in his world. Identifying the Dominant (D) or Submissive (S) horse in your pasture is quite easy. Merely throw out a pile of food or a series of piles of food and watch how they sort themselves out. Horses always have a pecking order. No two are exactly equal. They may only be separated by a tiny margin, but one will be above the other.

For our needs to sort horses into personalities, it is sometimes best to observe them in several different herd situations or to create one as we do in a clinic situation. The reason for this is that so many of our horses live in a very small herd, which will not always give us a clear reading. The boss may be the boss only because he has been there the longest and inherited the dominant position, not having worked for it. Try your horse in several group settings if you are uncertain. In a large herd (meaning ten or more horses) it will be very obvious.

You may try classifying them in their energy group first. Are they Lazy or Energetic (see Chapter 2)? If they are Dominant and fall into the Lazy category, and you make them go forward, they will tell you how they feel about it by swishing their tail, kicking out or bucking. If they are Submissive, even though Lazy, they will usually comply without too much fuss. If you know your horse is Energetic but unsure of whether he is Dominant or Submissive, again, observe how willingly he complies with your wishes. If you ask the Energetic Dominant horse to slow down when he does not want to, he will invariably respond with a bit of temper by pulling or rooting, even bucking or kicking out. Whereas the Energetic Submissive horse will just try to run away from everything, including you. He may gallop sideways, showing more nervousness and worry rather than anger.

The Dominant and Submissive horses may look similar, but understanding or feeling the emotion behind each (Energetic or Lazy) will help you categorize your horse.

What are they like?

Mr. Dominant wants control. He will eat and drink first, be first to come into the barn, be first through the gate or decide when it is time to go out to pasture. The Dominant horse can be a mare or gelding. If geldings, sometimes they will display stallion-like tendencies, stretching their necks out as they herd and move mares in the group or actually mounting them for breeding. That is your top horse. But the next in line will usually be waiting to be number one, and further down the line the D's will always be waiting to achieve a higher spot in the pecking order.

If they become boss, they are confident in the role. Most Dominant horses establish their dominance without a lot of fighting. They have a superior air about them and almost dare other horses to question their authority. As riders we can learn how to be good bosses by watching and learning from them. Being a good leader is not about squealing and kicking. They meet new horses face on and are ready for the challenge. We will encounter this same attitude occasionally as their trainers. We might be best to think of ourselves more as their life coaches rather than their bosses. The Dominant horse will respond much better to psychology than brute strength.

Submissive horses are content to be controlled. They feel comfortable with others making the decisions. They like to blend in, get along, not make waves, and avoid confrontation. They have patience and wait their turn to eat, drink or go through a gate. They appreciate being looked after. They carry a feminine, receiving type of energy.

In response to repeated stress in their lives, Dominant and Submissive horses react quite differently. Dominants carry a male, expressing type of energy so they tend to act out, while Submissives may internalize stress and thus end up with physical problems, especially back issues.

Sometimes extreme Submissive horses find themselves in a leadership role. They are not very good at it, nor are they really happy in that role. They can look a lot like us when we are trying to be dominant and in control. There will be a lot of noise and commotion, kicking and fussing. They feel insecure without a leader. Moderately Submissive horses are usually not good bosses. They act like bullies, always trying to prove they are the boss and harassing the bottom horses. This happens most often in a paddock situation where two Submissive horses are housed together, or in a herd that has been established for some time.

How does this affect our relationship?

If you want to truly understand how the two of you will relate to each other, you may begin by assessing how you feel about control. Do you need to be in control of situations all or most of the time? If so, working with Mr. Dominant will have some challenges as he feels the same way. If you can learn to give and take a little and allow him some freedom as to how he does things, you will make a confident, take-charge kind of team.

If, on the other hand, you cannot give up any of the control, the battles will rage on over simple issues and neither of you will be terribly happy. If the rider must win at all costs, the horse may turn off and become dull and obedient or go the other way and become a nervous, anxious horse because he never feels that he is being listened to or doing anything right. This same horse may thrive in the hands of amateurs or juniors because they allow him to make some decisions, actually depending on him in certain situations. The Big D's, with the Big egos, love that.

The rider who likes to be in control would be much more successful with a Submissive horse because Submissives love to be told what to do. This is what makes them feel safe in their world. They need you to be there for them every stride; they need you to be a leader for them. A Dominant horse will help you out if you are an insecure rider where the Submissive horse will dissolve into a puddle of insecurities if you are not there for them. This definitely does not mean you should sell your horse if you are the wrong match. Horses will always prompt us to examine our own lives and start to make changes. Once you know that your Submissive horse needs a leader in his life, you will have to step up to the plate and find your strength. As you become the leader he needs, you may be pleasantly surprised at a new person emerging in other situations.

The same goes for the Dominant/control pair. Allow the horse to teach you a new, more flexible and creative way to interact with others. By knowing what personality type your horse is, you can then change how you approach him so that both of you come away with a win/win feeling.

Chapter 2

Energetic or Lazy

Is your horse Energetic (E) or Lazy (L)? How much effort does your horse put into his work, his life and his play? Determining this will help you understand what your horse needs from you as well as what are reasonable expectations for you to have of him.

Observing horses in their turnout time will reveal what energy type they are and, consequently, how that will affect their other personality traits. Are they happy to hang around in the shed most of the day? Or do they like to go out exploring and trot off to investigate new things? Do they have crazy periods in the day where they burn circles around and around in their paddocks?

Youngsters who have not been started will be easy to assess in terms of which energy trait they possess by watching them in their play. Who initiates most of the running, chasing, playing, and keeps it going long after the others are tired? If you are looking for a prospect in a sport that requires a lot of energy, this is your horse. If you are looking for the novice or amateur horse, the baby you will most likely want to select will be the one that called it quits some time ago.

If you are riding your horse, you will know very easily which energy type your horse is by how much leg you need, or in contrast, how much hand you need. The easiest horse to work with is the one that is near the centre line, not too Energetic and not too Lazy.

What are they like?

Mr. Energetic is eager to get out and work, looks forward to your rides, and comes across as excited and enthusiastic. He may be impatient, pawing in the alley of the barn as you are tacking up, tromping about in circles when you go to mount, and head up and ready to go when you hit the saddle. You only need to think trot and you are off. Whatever pace you are in, they are eagerly awaiting the word to go faster.

E's have trouble learning to relax and to rate themselves (control their own pace). They generally learn more easily when they have had a long loose warm-up where they are able to burn off some of their steam. They are not horses that you can leave in a stall or paddock and ride once or twice a week—well, you can, but it will certainly not be a pleasure ride.

E's must be taught how to relax and release energy because more exercise just makes them more fit. Some ways to do this are: hind quarter yields or disengaging to redirect some of their power; teaching them to drop their heads using a cue; or encouraging them to go long and low. Lateral flexions and changes of direction are also good ways to dissipate some of the energy in a positive manner.

High energy usually comes with high sensitivity. And so a steady quiet leg will help E's to settle as well as having the added benefit of getting the rider out of a bracing position, which is very common when one consistently rides the "go" or E horse.

It is easy to get into using too much rein on these horses, but they will just build more and more energy the more they are held in. Using a circle to help them rate and then doing single rein flexions will relax them and get them into some rhythm. Energetic horses are hard to keep steady on the bit. They are inclined to be either behind the bridle or running through the bridle. An exercise that helps these horses is the following contact exercise. As part of your warm-up on this horse, ride with elastic arms and practice following wherever his head goes so that there is never a pull, blip or slack going down the rein. Start at the walk and wait until they can totally accept you being there before proceeding through the other paces. This acceptance is so important before you start to influence or ask the horse for more.

The initial stage of rhythm and relaxation is the longest and most difficult stage when training these horses. Once achieved, everything else will fly along as they will have ample impulsion and enthusiasm for advanced maneuvers.

Mr. Lazy is pretty content where he is at: sunning himself, loafing in the shed or snoozing in his stall. Does he really have to do more? Luckily, he is usually pleasant enough to go along with your agenda. Having a "long fuse" is another way to describe the positive qualities of this horse. It will take something fairly scary to set his feet moving. He IS a horse after all and still has a flight instinct—which he needs to survive—but the distance that he will flee will be much shorter than Mr. Energetic. The L horse will be turned around and already inspecting the worrisome object while the E horse will still be on the run.

This does make them somewhat safer, which may be why we find more L horses with novices or juniors. But be advised, how safe your horse is will be determined by his other personality traits as well. Lazy with Afraid and Aloof may be difficult to control. This horse is still going to spook and be afraid. Some L's when afraid are more inclined to buck than run away. They are often so quiet that it is hard to tell when they are afraid of something and they can easily get pushed beyond their comfort zone which is what usually initiates the bucking. In contrast, the Energetic horse would have let his rider know from fifty feet away that he was frightened and needed more time to process whatever was so scary.

Training, as always, is the key ingredient to building a solid horse. Motivating L's is your training challenge. Submissive when combined with Lazy will be easier to get to go forward than Dominant and Lazy. They will make you work for what you get. Spurs and whips can make them go. But challenge yourself to find positive ways to motivate them. Liking the sport or activity they do is sometimes enough, especially if they are Aloof. Clicker training is a positive reward program that is very successful with the horse that lacks motivation. It makes the training session much more fun for both of you (See "Tools").

L's will do well in activities where short bursts of energy are required. In sports where the slow-down and the stop are critical, a little bit of L is almost a prerequisite. L's will be able to think through intricate patterns and maneuvers. They have a strong sense of self preservation and that includes preserving their energy. These are not the horses that will run away and jump off cliffs. Unless terribly afraid, they are usually your quiet, steady horses.

How does this affect our relationship?

What are the other personality traits of your horse? Remember, the Energetic trait will magnify any of them. Is he the strong, dominant type? Is he bold and confident? Is he Afraid and Aloof? Look at these and then either add Energetic or Lazy to figure out how it will affect this individual. For example:

- Energetic with Afraid will be, "Run!", while Lazy with Afraid will be, "Stop, snort, I'm not going!"
- Energetic with Curious will be, "Cool, what's that? Let's go look at it."
- Energetic with Dominant will be, "I'm going!", while Lazy with Dominant will be "You can't make me."
- Energetic with Aloof will be, "I'm gone, catch me if you can." Energetic with Friendly will be, "Come on, it'll be fun!"

How will the understanding of these traits affect your training program? Does your horse need short, quick workouts (Lazy), or does he need to go out for a six mile trot before he is ready to settle in and learn his lessons (Energetic)? Understanding your horse's personality helps you know what he needs in his warm up as well as in other aspects of his life.

Which of these horses would be most suited for your personality? In general, looking to opposites is best. If you are a high energy, ultra communicative "A-type" individual, your energy will float Mr. Lazy along nicely. However, if you own Mr. Energetic, it may be best for you to take a yoga class before coming to the barn to ride or both of you will be bouncing through the rafters. If you are the laid-back, relaxed, no stress, no expectation type of person, Mr. Energetic may just melt into you and be able to settle and really be focused on giving you his all.

So you already own this horse and you are not the ideal match. What now? As usual, learn from it. This is your opportunity, your gift. If you both have the L trait, maybe you need to learn to get more excited and enthused about life and project more of who you are. Bring energy to the barn and see if you can ignite him. Do quick, fun, short workouts and see if you can light up his life.

Or perhaps you are a pair of mismatched E's thrust together. Try not to rush to the barn, late for your lesson, cell phone in one hand and planning all the things you need to do after your ride. This energy will ricochet around you and Mr. Energetic will be only too happy to pick up some of your energy as if he doesn't have enough already. Your high energy horse needs to learn to slow down and get balanced and centered, and that may be his gift for you. Try turning off the cell phone on the drive to the barn, playing some classical music, being early so you can take him out for a little graze or play or hack before work. Try staying in the moment and see how nice it feels for both of you.

Our relationship with our horse is an opportunity for us to learn and to grow. We just have to see it as our journey and enjoy the process.

Chapter 3

Curious or Afraid

How does your horse approach new things in his life? Is he the bold, curious one that has to touch everything new that he sees? Or is he the tentative one, hanging back, waiting for someone else to go first, waiting to see if they come back alive? Which type you have can easily be observed in the field. How do they react when a bag blows through or a deer comes by? Does their curiosity outweigh their fear? Assessing them in the herd environment is sometimes most accurate as a Curious (C) horse can make a game out of being spooky when they are being ridden— anything to break up the monotony of going around and around in circles.

Normally, Curious horses will not be overly spooky, will like new places and new things and will be excited about their learning. Maggie, an extremely Curious horse that I was riding in the mountains, showed me an excellent example of this. We came upon a group of mountain sheep a ways off of the trail. The other horses were snorting and staring. She initially did that as well but then her curiosity took over and she marched into the woods to check them out closer. This same horse was the first to discover that she could chase elk in the field.

The Afraid (A) horse will be very tentative in this type of situation. The jumps in the corner of the arena are harboring horse eating dragons. The wash rack is a tiger trap; a rope dragging on the ground is most certainly a snake—a very venomous one. The list could go on and on. If you own Mr. Afraid, you know only too well.

At either end of the spectrum, problems can arise. The crazy Curious guy may be the one that will frequently hurt himself while investigating something new. He missed the story about the cat and curiosity and how it ended. The horses in all categories that are the easiest to be around are the ones that are close to the middle, not over the top at either extreme.

What are they like?

Mr. Curious is mentally active. He loves interaction on all levels. He likes to figure things out himself and may resent or at least get bored with the rider who feels the need to show him how to do everything. He is creative. If we are not playing games that engage him, he will probably invent a few of his own, even spooky games to see if he can get a rise out of us. In the negative, they can find numerous ways to push our buttons. In the positive, they are engaging and anxious to learn new things.

Even out in the barn or field they are opening gates, eating blankets, demolishing their feed tubs or buckets, all in the name of entertaining themselves. To enjoy them, we must learn to engage their C trait. Schooling and training every day will leave them cold. They learn quickly and bore just as quickly. They love variety and going to new places. Sports that are challenging and have a lot of variety are the best for this type. Make up games to play—they love clicker training, in-hand games can also be fun. Set up your own horse agility course. What about poles, walking on a tarp, across a bridge? Try backing in an L or running a barrel racing pattern. On the trail, why not meander through the bush or circle back to go around the big rock; play hide and seek with your trail riding friends. In the field, use the hay bales to make up an interesting pattern or run some relays with your friends. The Curious horse will inspire you to be more creative and quit taking life so seriously.

Mr. Afraid is mentally active too, but he has somewhat of an overactive imagination. There is danger at every corner in his world. His flight instinct is ready to kick in at a moment's notice. This is where energy levels will factor in to quite a degree. Lazy and Afraid is obviously much easier to deal with than Energetic and Afraid. Whether Energetic or Lazy though, the Afraid horse needs to be kept safe. For Submissive and Afraid horses, what they need us to say is, "I will be there for you every stride." For Dominant and Afraid horses it will be, "I will not force you to deal with things that you are not ready for. If you are afraid I will give you lots of time."

The training of the Afraid horse is really the opposite of the Curious horse. They love repetition. Once they feel safe with us and their environment, they will perform their tasks for us consistently. They do not need a lot of entertaining. All they need is to be listened to and allowed to learn slowly and correctly. Certain sports demand a lot of focus, and the A is the personality trait that will help them put the hours in that are needed to learn a highly technical sport. Dressage or reining would be examples. Some horses are required to do the same job day in and day out. This is where you need the Afraid. Sports where it may be helpful to have an A might be team roping, barrel racing, pleasure show horses or trail riding.

The Curious horse in these sports would be constantly trying to find a way to make the job more interesting. If you own a C and do one of these sports, it merely means that you need to get them out doing other things any chance you can. Remember, Curious is all about variety, and Afraid is all about routine.

How does this affect our relationship?

Would you be compatible with an Afraid horse? Begin by analyzing your personality. Do you allow fear to sneak into your life and restrict you from time to time? Do you, like your Afraid horse, have an overactive imagination and can conjure up vivid accidents in CSI detail at a moment's notice? If so, the two of you may feed off of each other. You may be TOO understanding of his fears, wanting to mother him, coddle and protect him. This is usually not in either of your best interests.

If you tend to be a worried rider and you have had a negative experience with an Afraid horse, to restore your confidence in riding, you may have to ride another horse at least for awhile—one that carries more of his own confidence. He could be an Afraid horse as long as he has been well-trained. Most times we can work through the problem with the Afraid horse by following a very structured, consistent program that we slowly build on over time. That is what they are seeking—consistency. Approach a problem with this horse by setting a doable goal and then fill in ten steps on how to get there. This horse wants you to have that type of program for all of his training.

The rider who has some fear issues can be successful with an Afraid horse by providing a consistent training program—something that would likely come naturally. As a pair you will both love routine, order, and a well executed plan. Neither will be bored with the miles or the circles that the program demands.

If you are more the Curious type—you like exploring new ideas, love change, love travel, find repetitive tasks boring, more likely to be known for your spontaneity than your follow through—then you will find the Curious horse right up your alley. Doing a different thing every day of the week will suit both of you. Remember that if the horse you own is not your match, all you need to do is vary your riding program.

Chapter 4

Friendly or Aloof

Nearly everyone thinks that their horse is friendly. We would all like to believe that they love us and are as involved in the relationship as we are. You will know if your horse is truly Friendly (F) if he hangs around when loose even if you do not have any treats or rewards for him. The Aloof (A) horse will usually scope you out and then say "see you later" if there is no reward in it for him, especially if you have offended him recently in any way. When catching them in the field they are prone to making you walk the distance.

Mr. Friendly loves to be petted and touched and groomed, while Mr. Aloof could care less about any contact unless he has a spot that needs to be scratched. Grooming, he only tolerates. If you observe the horses in the field, you will find Mr. Friendly surrounded by friends. He will greet them vocally and be very involved with many relationships, while Mr. Aloof will not be terribly chatty and may be off by himself a good part of the day.

Most Friendly horses will be interested and ready to interact with a new person, while the Aloof horse will be a bit wary or indifferent. How extreme these traits are and how they play out with the other characteristics will determine what type of horse you have.

What are they like?

Mr. Friendly is personable, very interactive, and communicative. He is trying to figure you out, and usually trying to please you. He loves attention. When Friendly is combined with the Submissive trait in a horse, he is usually described as sweet and soft. Or when combined with Dominant, a horse will be cute and cuddly, sometimes even cheeky and sassy. However they do it, they will get your attention. They need to be appreciated for everything they do. They need to be told how fabulous they are. They need the relationship.

Mr. Aloof is the introvert. Because he is a horse he will not want to be totally alone as he still needs the herd to feel safe. But you will find him on the fringe of most activities. If he is Dominant in the herd, the Aloof horse will take his role very seriously and perhaps be more bossy than required. They take themselves seriously. They take their work seriously and can be the horse equivalent of a workaholic. They are interested in little else. Even the relationship is serious. Fun and frivolity is not a high priority in their lives, they need to have meaning in what they do.

When Aloof is combined with Curious, you get a much more outgoing horse, but still usually on their own terms. Rather than one sport they will be happiest participating in several, all of their own choosing.

This attachment to the job makes the Aloof horse very valuable. He does not need a lot of coaching and help with his job once he has learned it. If he likes it, he is happy to go do it; happy to repeat the performance over and over. For this reason, you will sometimes see the Aloof horse (particularly if the horse is also Curious) passed from one Junior rider to the next. They can really show you how to get the job done.

How does this affect our relationship?

As usual, keeping a relationship healthy and working in the positive is more about listening than talking. With Mr. Friendly it is easy to carry on a conversation. But what about Mr. Aloof? What does he want from us? Sometimes we feel like he doesn't need us at all. His independence can be frustrating to us if we are in this for the relationship. We may need to look at our partnership on his terms and not ours. If we need a lot of warm, fuzzy, contact, we perhaps should get a dog. This horse is not going to fill our needs in that role.

But we can still enjoy him on many other levels. He is happy to work, takes pride in his job and will be very pleased to share that part of his life with us. Aloof horses usually appear friendly and loyal to their grooms, trainers or riders. They bond with them because these are the people that allow them to express themselves. That expression is through their work. If we have an Aloof horse in our lives, it says it is time to get to the job, to put the analyzing and psychology on the shelf, to quit talking and just go do the work.

Section II

The Personality Types

Chapter 5

DECF   The Rock Star

Lights! Camera! Action! The Rock Star loves to be in the limelight. They have the cool confidence to pull off feats that would leave most horses quaking in their horseshoes. They love the attention from beginning to end. They love to have an entourage following them around making sure everything is in order for their performance. They tolerate all the fussing that goes with getting them ready for the show, whether it is braids or bathing—whatever the sport dictates. Once they walk into the ring, the world is theirs. With daring speed, dazzling strength or perfect precision they perform to the absolute utmost of their ability—no holds barred. They love the competition. They expect the fans to be there with hands in the air cheering them on. When they walk out of the arena, a standing ovation would be fitting. It may not be the Olympics, but they have probably given an Olympic performance. If the only podium they stand on is the one in your heart, that is fine with this personality.

The DECF has a strong ego, bordering on cocky, but personable and charming enough to endear them to you. The world revolving around them is as it should be. Their feed schedule, their exercise program—they expect you to have that on the top of your to-do list. They like to come first whether it is in the arena or around the farm. They are near the top of the pecking order with their herd mates and expect to be there with you as well. They have endless energy, which is most often positively expressed. Always eager and ready to go to work, they will meet you at the gate most days. They are curious and outgoing, definitely not shy, and will tell you how they feel about most things.

They love a challenge whether it is mental or physical. This quality results in them getting bored easily. Six days of schooling will really turn them off your sport. Because they are curious, variety is a key factor in training them. It also means that they are not your "fraidy cats." If something startles or scares them, they will almost appear embarrassed to have jumped or acted flighty like those other lesser herd mates. This horse is your friend and noble companion. Most of what they do, they do for you and they love that you appreciate them. The Rock Star wants to live large and along the way enjoy freedom, fun and friendship.

Training

As a young horse going into training, you will be impressed with the amount of confidence that the DECF has. You will be challenged by their "big D", as they will be testing whether you really are a dominant factor in their life. Some days they are "just too cool for school," as a trainer friend expressed one day about a three year-old that she was starting. In general, they like to run the show, so initially setting the ground rules can have its challenges, although their willingness to learn and please will usually override that willfulness as long as you appreciate their effort. They must be kept physically active and mentally engaged. The trainer that can keep this horse's ego and confidence intact through the initial training will be well rewarded down the road when he gets into his performance years.

This is not a horse to fight with over small issues at any age. He is friendly and engaging, seeking the relationship with you. He is willing to work with you on most issues.

Over-disciplining will get him worried or "on the fight" and you may lose your superstar. Do not allow him to push you around but do allow him a few of his own ideas. This is not the horse that needs to be told where to put every foot. He has his own confidence. Once he understands his sport or job, he will be only too happy to perform it for you. He may even show you some innovative ways on how it could be done bigger and better and faster. This is a horse to be listened to—he has something to say!

Once DECF's have their training or careers in place, they make great horses for the amateur, junior or rider that is lacking confidence. This horse has enough confidence for both of you. He can be loved on extensively without taking serious advantage of you. As long as you are out there playing and performing with them and catering to their every wish, they will make a fabulous, trustworthy companion. They look out for themselves and will look after you. You will be able to leave him for the winter and when you climb on in the spring he will be safe, solid and happy to get back at it.

As a pleasure horse or trail riding horse, they will love to be the one that can lead the others through danger. Whether it is boggy ground, a high flowing creek, or strange animals on the trail, his first reaction is: "Step aside little lady, the Rock Star is here."

Retirement is hard for this regal horse. Some decline rapidly when turned out to pasture. They have loved being in service, so they find it hard to slow down. When they are finished their active show career, being a family pleasure horse or trail riding horse may satisfy their needs for a few years. Keeping them going as long as possible may be best. Again it will be about listening to them. They will tell you how they feel. Some Rock Stars will be far too proud to be the kid's horse. For them, remaining in their herd as the leader may be the healthiest option.

Careers

The Rock Star is found excelling in most competitive arenas. Their enthusiasm will tell you what sports they like. Don't just stick to one. They will be happier doing a wide range of activities as long as they know them well enough to be proficient at them. The rider's capabilities will ultimately determine the DECF's level of performance. They are not your perfectionists. But their egos say they like to be competent at what they do. They have difficulty in repetitive jobs or ones that require lots of schooling and not a lot of limelight. If this horse has come into your life, it is time to widen your horizons and go play!

Chapter 6

DECA The Macho Man

If this horse could wear colors, he would. He would hit the open road on a Harley with a devil-may-care attitude. These cocky horses handle any new job with ease. They'll tell you how it should be done and do it efficiently and quickly. And when they are done, don't make a big fuss over them. Save your accolades for someone else. They are in it for the sport. Hugs and praise are just going to annoy them. Yes, they want to be appreciated—but please, do it in a dignified manner. DECA's love the challenge, and the more you throw at them, the better. You will find these horses in the competition arena, usually still fighting with their owners about how it should have been done and then grumbling all the way to the winner's circle.

The Macho Man can be described as "tough" in both the positive and negative sense of the word. In the positive, it might mean being a "tough" competitor, never giving up, determined to cross the finish line. In the negative, it might mean fighting with you all day about an issue. This horse is pure determination, usually determined to do it his way. When doing what they love, they are enthusiastic go-getters. Get out of their way and let them perform.

Training

The Macho Man is the strong, silent type. He demands respect. He gets it in the pasture and expects it from you. Some trainers have a hard time with this view point and feel they must dominate this strong individual. Years of resistance and fighting may follow. Know that this horse can be a top competitor because they love the job. And so your job needs to be to find the Macho Man his job.

The challenge in training them initially is allowing *them* to do things their way. It may take a lot of psychology to teach them while they think they are teaching you. The Aloof factor in their personality is your blessing. This personality wants, even needs, a job. Once you find something that they like, they want to work at it. It may mean incorporating it into their routine every day. They will put up with a few boring circles as long as it leads to what they like to do. That may be jumping, cows, trail riding, barrel racing. It will usually have an outward focus as they are not the horse that is into pleasing you—that is left for the Friendly horse. Getting through the early years of training is hard as the Macho Man is all too eager to rush off into the job with only half the skills.

A trainer friend had a particularly challenging project— a young Warmblood mare named Coco who was a DECA with extremely Dominant and Curious traits in her personality. Every day she could come up with another way NOT to participate in the training process—not being caught, not leading, not steering, not trotting, and so on. After studying the personality, the trainer knew she couldn't fight with her and would have to find a way to work with her. The Aloof trait and its attachment to job might be the secret she theorized. She realized that the mare was bred to jump so decided to try her out. She loved it. She then incorporated it into her riding sessions even though the mare was barely trotting and up until then could not be ridden where you wanted to go. Each day the trainer would set up little courses of poles and x's to jump. Coco would jump with enthusiasm and canter away as happy as could be. This mare was only three years old and already a "point and go" type of jumper. The schooling she needed was tactfully slipped in here and there. The next year a teenage girl bought her and the two of them were happily doing 1.10 meter (3' 6") courses by the end of her four year-old year.

The Macho Man horse normally carries a lot of his own confidence, if anything TOO much. The E and C (Energetic and Curious) tell us they will express how they feel. And in the DECA, because the E and C are mixed with the Dominant trait, what they express is usually not what you want to hear. The curious says they like to figure things out on their own. As we saw from the previous story this can be a challenge in the beginning. Finding ways to work with them so that they can get a job they like at an early stage is of the utmost importance.

Another Macho Man that I knew did an amazing number of tricks. He was a pinto named Cloudy with a big number branded on his hip. His young owner started him herself, and his tricks developed because she would reward him for what other more experienced horse people would have reprimanded him for. One day, chasing cows, she was whistling to move the cows and he didn't like it so he bucked. She, being a child and as Curious as him, decided it was fun and rewarded him for it. Years later, he would still buck on command any time she whistled. It was an especially great trick when others were riding him!

In much the same way, she taught him to rear when she put her legs ahead on him. One year she was riding him in the Calgary Stampede Parade and was showing off his new rearing trick at every stop on the parade route. To her chagrin the announcer commented that this young girl was having a lot of trouble "controlling" her horse.

I met this horse in his later years, and he was still spunky and full of life, pleased to show off his tricks. I was told he could still be a runaway if the notion overcame him— never a dangerous one as he was always aware of where he was going. His owner enjoyed years of fun simply by appreciating who he was and by doing almost every horse sport there was. That's the way to ride a Macho Man.

If your Macho Man has not had this ideal upbringing and his attitude has turned negative—usually from a trainer being too controlling and fighting with him—then you are in for serious resistance. The C and A (Curious and Aloof) say they are not looking for a friend and therefore can be very creative in finding ways to test you at times, almost appearing to have a sense of humor about your unfortunate situation.

They love playing games. But not your touchy-feely ground games—more the "what can I get you to do" type of games, sometimes not being caught, sometimes acting spooky and afraid. This is a surprising and interesting one of their games, especially effective at undermining your confidence. If you have bought this horse, then your challenge will be to quit trying to train him. Help him find his job and allow him to show you how it should be done. Then, sit down, shut up and hold on. They will take you for a ride. Enjoy it!

Careers

The DECA horse can excel at any competitive sport. They may be a show jumper, a bucking horse, a cow horse, an endurance horse, a rodeo horse, a games horse, a polo horse, a ranch horse, or a three-day event horse (perhaps a Murphy himself but the dressage part will definitely not be his forte.) Exciting sports are fine with this personality.

The DECA is not your typical pleasure horse. If you only ride once or twice a month and like to "tootle," good luck. This horse needs a lot of exercise mentally and physically. If they are not being challenged in a positive way, they will challenge us in a negative way.

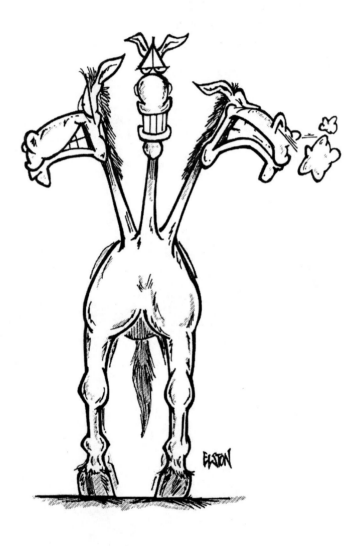

Chapter 7

DEAF   The Wild Card

If you are a card player you understand the wild card. One comes into your hand and you are ecstatic. It means you receive bonus points or you can use it to substitute for another card—all good. Then once in a while you get "caught" with the wild card in your hand at the end of the game. This is never good—usually costing BIG points against you. So how do we feel about the Wild Card horse? Most of the time, we love them. But we must be ever mindful for they can turn on us if we are not careful.

The DEAF, or Wild Card horse, has the same unpredictability. Most of the time, so loveable, cute and friendly. But occasionally, they can turn around on you and suddenly you have an overbearing monster on your hands. Their cuteness can have a manipulative side to it. They will stand just that little bit too close, sort of in your face. You may see it as just friendly until they push it to the next stage, and you move back or give ground in some way and they smugly say, "Gotcha." They have just taken the upper hand.

This might not be a problem if they carried their own self confidence like some of the other Dominants. But this personality has the fear gene running through it. If they are left on their own, fear starts to overcome training. You understand they need help and lack confidence so you try to take control of them and the situation. Their big D does not appreciate this. You have just released the monster. It might be angry, afraid, impulsive, even explosive. It needs to be wrestled back into its cage. But how?

DEAF—the letters of this personality describe them very well. Listen? You want me to listen? They are dominant and strong-minded with a lot of energy. Now what do you think happens when you add fear to that? You are going to have to fight, even to have your idea heard. They can be emotional, even hot. These guys can take over and "check out of Dodge." When they do, self preservation is not one of their strong suits. They do not always slow down and think things through. This personality can shatter a good rider's confidence and a novice should probably not be near them.

The successful horses in this category were ridden for most of their early years by a professional. The part of their personality that creates most of the problem for amateurs is, surprisingly enough, the Friendly. Most of us are suckers for the friendly, cute, funny face. We want that in our horses. The problem arises because we give away too much, we want them to like us, or we are just unaware of how subtle the sign was. Before we know it, the Wild Card has stepped across the line, and because he did it in a "cute" way, we let him get away with it. This is a slippery slope, and it is very hard to gain that ground back after we have given it away.

The Afraid needs you to take control of the situation, needs you to be the leader, needs you to show them how to behave. The Dominant says that you will need to do that quietly and calmly for them to listen. If you start shouting, they will as well. The Friendly says they love attention; your challenge is to honor that without giving up your power. The Energetic and Friendly traits say ride me, lots. Most E's and F's are sensitive and will anticipate every little signal and aid and be bouncing to do it before you think you have asked.

In the positive, this horse is very generous. Learning to honor his generosity without compromising your strength is important. Yes, ride them lots, but in an environment where they feel safe. For them to feel safe they need a rider that is quiet, firm and fair. This IS the way we are doing it. Do not fight with them—they have a lot of energy and attitude if you want to go there. They love routine and will thrive on what other ponies find absolutely tedious. Once they feel safe in their world, they will love to show off and be on center stage just like the other DEAF's.

Training

Boundaries, boundaries, boundaries! With the Wild Card, the best way to establish boundaries is with a solid base of ground work, even if he has come into your life as a "going" horse. It is usually on the ground where he starts to take over control. Dominant leading (See "Tools") is a good starting point that you will probably go back to many times in your training.

In the barn or tied in the alley you must be ever vigilant that he must not step into your space. Most DEAF's are "trompers"—quite happy to tromp into you, even over you when they get distracted. Keeping their attention on you or a task at hand is of the utmost importance. These horses in a herd must always be aware of the leader and to keep this horse feeling safe he must know that you are the leader.

The Friendly factor is what makes him a bit of an enigma. You can cuddle and love on him but within the boundaries of leadership. Do it on your terms, not his. You cannot love him into being well-behaved. This horse, if he were a person, would probably be the sweet talker. He can easily slip into your space and then start to take it over. Horses establish dominance by getting the other horses to move. Be careful that you do not step back and give ground to him when he steps into you.

Most of us are not even aware we are doing it. This subtle move will start his mind thinking that if he can get you to step back here, he can start to boss you. If your leadership is not well-established on the ground, it will start to erode in your riding. It may be a small incident of perhaps not listening to your leg that then can become blowing out on a circle or even bucking and running off. Some of the undesirable behaviors are done from dominance and others are from fear. Either way, it is imperative that you go back to a control situation where they understand that you are the leader in no uncertain terms.

A good leadership exercise is playing with him in the round pen. Make sure you can send him away from you and draw him back to you on YOUR terms. With his Dominant trait you will begin to see him want to dictate the rules. He may show his anger and attitude when you send him away by bucking or kicking out at you or simply being sticky and refusing to go. His next move to try and dominate the situation will be drawing back into you with the cutest of all expressions before you have actually asked for the draw. Your relationship will be off to a good start when you can send him away quietly at the walk, and he will walk and wait for you to ask him to come into you and then will stand a respectful distance from you when he stops. At this point he can have the petting and loving that he so desperately wants—always on your terms.

Ground driving or long lining is also an excellent exercise to establish dominance with the Wild Card. He needs to be sent out of your space and this gives you the added advantage of still being able to put him to work in a constructive way. He learns that you are there for him and can help keep him safe and then he can let go of his resistance to you controlling him. Too much energy can be a problem with the DEAF. Long lining will give you a positive way to help dissipate some of it as well as helping him find rhythm and balance.

When schooling this horse, they like patterns and routines. Consistency is so important. Don't change the program. Don't change the sport. Change is upsetting for them, so you must prepare them well to go into new situations. If you decide to try a new sport or job, keep your expectations low and allow them to do it frequently until they truly understand it. As a rider you may think that going on a mountain trail ride might be a real pleasure for your horse—like a holiday. Instead it may be very upsetting if he hasn't done it before. If you want to go into a new territory, it is important that you make a commitment to it, planning to do it every day for a week or two or until he really understands it and can be happy in that environment. This is how he builds trust in your relationship. They are not horses that get bored easily, so the pay off is that once they get it, they will be happy to give you a 120 percent every day and do the job repeatedly. All they need is you to appreciate them, honor their Friendly and keep them safe.

In the herd, the DEAF will always be trying to move up in the pecking order, if they are not already at the top. Just as they are with us, they are always waiting for the door of opportunity to open so they can step in and gain a little ground. Not only do we get sucked in by their cute friendly demeanor, but the other horses do as well. They will approach other horses in a playful friendly manner and then instantly strike out and get in a bite. They are extremely social, even to the point of being sticky and overly friendly with other herd mates. In our herd we have a very Aloof, Submissive Perfectionist (SEAA) who is old and prefers to be well away from the social activities of the herd. But to his chagrin, our new DEAF decided that he liked him as his friend and followed him everywhere, wanting to touch and groom him even though the old man kept trying to get away from him.

The DEAF can become very bonded with other horses and be extremely emotional when separated. When we can be the leader that they need, they can then share that same strong bonding with us.

If you are a soft, submissive type of person, this horse will teach you to build some solid boundaries and learn how to define and defend them. If you are the strong dominant type and have drawn this horse into your life, maybe you are being asked to throw down your sword and learn to lead with quiet confidence.

Careers

Any job where you are there for them one hundred percent of the time will be fine with them. They are more like the Submissive horses in this way. Patterns work well because they love predictability and need to be told exactly what to do. If they can perform the same task over and over again and have you appreciate what they are doing, then they are in their happy place.

These horses do not need to be a competitive horse, but they do need a lot of riding and a consistent program so it will only work for them as long as their rider is very dedicated. A pleasure horse they are not. Riding three or four times a month will make both partners pretty frustrated and unhappy. They will have too much energy, too much attitude (D), too much fear (seeing horse eating monsters everywhere) and you will wonder what happened to your Friendly guy. They would be happy trail horses as long as you ride frequently and like to put on lots of miles. The Sunday pleasure ride with family and neighbors will not be a pleasure.

A large group of horses in any environment will make it a challenge for them to listen to you. To handle that type of situation you will need a lot of well-established cues and programming to keep their attention on you. If you let their attention wander, in no time they will be trying to pass someone, trying to bully someone or spooking at every unusual object.

They are definitely not the beginner horse until they are in their senior years. At that point in their life they can have so much to offer because they are friendly and want to please. They will still have good energy to offer, so that beginners will not feel that they are riding the "old plug." Even then, they will still need to be kept in a familiar environment where they will feel safe. They always have been friendly and wanted to please. It was just that their energy and fear took them over the top where they couldn't listen.

Endurance racing might be right up their alley, with lots of miles to burn energy and a consistent partner with which to do it. They would not get bored with all the training miles.

They would have show presence and like the routine of sports such as reining, dressage or quadrille. They love to show off all the things they know—that is the D's ego. Their rider would need to have a pact with them: I will keep you safe; you turn over the control to me. The degree to which they could do that would be the degree to which they could be successful. DEAF's are not your "jack of all trades." Pick one sport and help them perform it.

Once the DEAF is working for you, he has ample energy and expression that he will freely give to any situation or sport. You will truly feel that you are blessed to have a Wild Card in your hand.

Chapter 8

DEAA   The Boss

The Boss takes life and his job seriously. Come along for the ride if you like. Not unlike some of our bosses in the human world, there will be times when you will do most of the work and they will be there to take more of the glory, even act like they did it all themselves.

The DEAA can be emotional. He will express it. Just like your human boss, you will know what you did wrong. It may have been pushing him into a new territory that he wasn't ready for, holding to a rigid plan, having to be right, or meeting his attitude with your attitude. He will show his ire at any of these misdemeanors. You will learn, the boss can be emotional, you must never be.

Their ego needs constant pampering. They can be arrogant and controlling. What we have here are leaders with fear issues. They expect you to get it right and will not be very forgiving if you mess it up. The Boss is not a kid's horse even if he is a pony. He does not have a sentimental nurturing side, nor is he likely to develop one. Don't give these guys a hug or tell them they are cute. They are dignified and proud and want you to respect them at all times.

Their personality is much like the DECA's (Macho Man) because of the Dominant and Aloof similarities. But when we add the Afraid factor, we get a bit of a conflicted personality. On the trail they hate to be at the back of the ride because they are Dominant. But put them out front and they become spooky. Similarly in the herd, they want to be the boss, but they are not necessarily a good boss—or at least not a good leader—because they are afraid to be out front. They want to be the cocky bold one but really need others to help them pull it off. And don't expect gratitude for it! Like the DECA's they need their jobs but these guys need quite a bit of help with them. They act like they are ultra confident but then have a meltdown if something surprises them.

"I'm a great jump horse, this course is so easy. (Whoa, stop, spook, shy...) Who put that Liverpool there?!"

And they hate to be caught in a weak moment. To avoid this it is best for the DEAA's to stay in the same job. The Boss is a bit of a perfectionist, so he doesn't mind doing something repetitively as long as he is doing well at it. He is not a jack of all trades. Let him learn his job and stay with it. He can't look good if he is in the process of learning something—and looking good is important to these guys.

Focusing on their jobs really helps them keep on track, especially if the job has an outside focus like working cows, jumping or barrels. Think of them needing a career. The AF's (Afraid and Friendly) can look to you for your input every step of the way and feel safe, but the AA's (Afraid and Aloof) can get annoyed with us if we have too much input. They like to call the shots. They don't have a soft spot and they can't be fooled, so we need to be really up front with them.

Most DEAA's that fall through the cracks haven't been given a job that they can do well. They are not "triers" who keep struggling to figure out what we want. Without a job and meaning in their lives, they can be angry and impulsive and even appear to resent your relationship. "Feed me and leave me alone," may be your only meeting ground.

The successful ones have usually done the same job all their lives, are quite good at it and take pride in it. You may feel at times that you are merely a means for them to go to work. For example, these horses may be the ones that will run over you to get into the trailer. At our barn, a DEAA jump pony dragged his little owner down the alley way of the barn when he saw the trailer doors open at the back door. We were trying to load a more difficult horse and the little Boss barged right by us and went in dragging his shank! "Let's get this show on the road!"

Training

Start DEAA's early and show them what their job is. They will love routine as long as they do not feel you are drilling them. They have a lot of energy and need to be worked regularly and seriously. Most DE's will thrive in a competitive home. Because they are Afraid, they need to be allowed to learn quietly and safely.

Some of these horses need safety circles for a long time to get settled before they can branch out and feel safe. A safety circle is simply a circle that you ride in the same place every time until it is the place where they feel comfortable and safe. From there, venture out slowly into a larger world, knowing that any time they become worried you have somewhere to go back to where they feel secure. For example, an owner of a very difficult DEAA did so many circles out in her field when she first bought her mare that the neighbor's thought the patterns were alien crop circles. This little Hanoverian mare went on to become a solid three-day event horse. The circle gave this rider a safe place from which to start.

Ground work is valuable for DEAA's for the same reason. They require firm boundaries. But always be a fair boss. Because of their A (Afraid) characteristic, they are more like Submissive horses in that they need to know that you are their leader to feel safe. Doing this with strong boundaries as opposed to aggressiveness is vital as they will meet aggression with aggression. In other words, be aware that you can not force your dominance on them. In fact, they will get emotional if you fight or bully them and they will block whatever you are trying to do. Don't overlook their sensitivity. They have the ability to be aware of very subtle cues.

Once your DEAA knows his job, you will want to allow him some latitude in how he does it. In a job they like and know well, DEAA's can function on auto pilot. At this point in their career, with solid years behind them, they may finally be ready to be the novice or junior horse.

The DEAA's that have not had a solid consistent start have probably gone from home to home. If they have been mishandled or abused in any way, they will hold on to their issues with a vengeance. These horses are not your forgiving type. They are strong and dominant whether angry or frightened. Repairing the damage with them can be a life sentence, but nonetheless rewarding when you see the hardness and anger give way to softness.

This horse can fall between the cracks because he can be too unpredictable for the amateur, and professionals realize that they are not a quick fix and may not be worth their time. Owners can be unforgiving of their attitude and undesirable behaviors, and therefore the DEAA's can easily be sent down the road. Selling them is frequently seen as an acceptable option because these horses, not having the Friendly gene, have not given their owners a lot of "warm fuzzies." Owners do not feel particularly bonded to them.

The Boss is the horse that the amateur will sometimes buy because they feel sorry for him and see him as misunderstood. This is the horse that is sometimes given to you because "you have the patience and skill to deal with him." If you are a softy and fell for this like I did with Tony the Pony, you probably have one happily eating out in your field and are not sure what to do with him now.

If you do have the time and patience to take on the project—and it is a project—of re-schooling a DEAA, the success will be relative to how quickly you can find him a job he likes and then allow him to do it. You will need to let go of agenda and expectation as this horse can smell those nasty human traits a mile away. Estimate three years to start. If you accept the challenge, know that the project won't be easy and success won't be quick. But the rewards of turning him around will be great. And along the way you will learn a lot as DEAA's have a knack for pushing our buttons and making us explore our emotions. These horses will challenge our training program until we finally learn to work **with,** rather than against, their dominance. This learning will then help us work with all other Dominants that we may have in our lives. These guys will demand we learn to use psychology rather than force.

Careers

As mentioned previously, the Boss prefers doing one job and one job well. Consider the following careers: cow work, jumping, ranch work, distance riding, three-day eventing, or combined driving (although they are probably not confident enough for a single). They respond best with a job that has a purpose and makes sense to them.

Retirement in the sense of being turned out in the field with the herd is not difficult for these horses. They will enjoy trying to boss the other horses around for the rest of their days.

Chapter 9

DLCF   The Reluctant Rock Star

The Reluctant Rock Stars are happy to perform. They like the travel and the attention and the fanfare. They love the special treatment and being pampered, but it takes a whole entourage for them to be on that center stage. They have to be managed and motivated to get there. The entourage will probably have to put up with quite a lot of resistance along the way. There will be days they have to be made to drag their butts out of their stalls.

Once out and working though, theses horses are your confident good boys. They try very hard for you. They are sensitive, kind, and pleasant to be around and will be totally forgiving. DLCF's will keep on going and giving even when they are sore or being mistreated. Stoic comes to mind. Most Dominants will not put up with much mishandling as they are only too happy to fight, but in these horses it is balanced out by the Lazy and the Friendly. They don't want to put in too much effort, and they do want to be liked. The D here seems to give them strength without a lot of attitude.

The DLCF is very similar to the DECF (Rock Star), without being quite so strong-minded. The main difference is in their energy levels. Reluctant Rock Stars are Lazy and need to be motivated. They have the strength and the confident persona, but the rider or trainer will have to be very goal-oriented in order to make it happen. The rider has to create motion and give it some direction. The response will probably be: "Don't push me—I'm going." But this horse will never be extremely willful or rebellious because he cares too much. They want the friendship. The DECF's are dying to show off, whereas the DLCF's have to be made to do the job. But then they love the praise and attention just as much. They perform more for the relationship than for the glory.

The personality of the Reluctant Rock Star was evident in a Standardbred breeding stallion that we had at the stable. He exemplified it in his breeding style. Most stallions used for hand breeding have rather a "slam dunk" kind of style. But this big fellow preferred to court. He would spend considerable time nibbling and talking to the mares. He knew about foreplay. They had to want him. He could only perform if everything was right. His time in the breeding shed was four times as long as the other stallion. He was a bit of a loud screamer when being led to the mare, and one day a cranky handler disciplined him. That was the end of breeding for that day. He lost all interest. So we see yet again the sensitive performer who needs you on his side.

Training

In general, this horse is an easy horse to train, because he wants to please you so much. An added benefit is his confidence and curiosity. He is not likely to be the dangerous type as he is not flighty. He would much rather get along than create problems. This horse will need creative approaches to learning because he is Curious. So mix up his workouts. He finds work a bit of a "drudgery drew" anyway so try to make it fun for him. This horse, if drilled constantly, will start to tune out and gloss over depending on the severity of the training. Negative training with this horse will create a quiet passive resistance. If they are not being listened to, they will start to shut down either physically or emotionally.

A wonderful mare named Wildwood, who was boarded at our barn, is a perfect example. She is a Hanoverian and not the modern, ultra refined type. When leading her out to her paddock, I would hear her clomping down the alley of the barn behind me, slow and reluctant, sounding like she weighed at least 2000 pounds. Later in the day I would stare in wonderment as I watched her and her petite owner doing dressage out in the grass ring. This same horse was lightly skipping across the ground doing tempe changes and beautiful floating half passes. She competed at high level dressage. Her owner worked out on a regular basis to give her the strength she needed to get this mare to the show ring. Once there they shone.

One year Wildwood's owner's career was taking precedence, and she debated whether she could show without doing the schooling required for dressage. She hired a young girl at the barn who hacked her out and just exercised her three to four times a week. When the owner came out for the one or two schools a week that she could fit in, she said the mare had never been so responsive—anxious to get doing the fun stuff, showing off every move she knew. It ended up being the ideal program for the Reluctant Rock Star. No drilling, little schooling, two people to dote on her and still able to show off in her sport.

The Lazy attribute in this horse attracts many riders who get worried when dealing with horses that have big energy. What attracts them to the Lazy is that they are quiet. What we have to then watch for is that we do not begin to resent them for exactly the characteristics that attracted us to them in the first place. Yes, he is Lazy.

How can I motivate him and enjoy him in a positive way? This horse loves to please. Stroke his ego—show him how fabulous he can be. Focus on what he is doing well rather than thinking of what he is not giving you. A small shift in thought process can make a huge difference in outcome.

Careers

The Reluctant Rock Star horse will be happy doing anything that pleases you. They can be your pleasure horse at home on your acreage, or your competitive companion. They will perform in the same arenas as the Rock Star, with the only difference being the amount of work you are putting in. Combined driving, dressage, cow work, pleasure, trail horse, reining, rodeo, jumping—they will love to do a variety of jobs excelling as the all-round horse. DLCF's make great teachers in the competitive arena once they know their job as they are confident and solid. Novice or junior riders can be safe, learn a new skill and enjoy a meaningful relationship with this horse.

Chapter 10

DLCA   The Prize Fighter

The Prize Fighter has a big ego, likes being in the ring, and wants to come out the winner. Problems arise if he sees you as his opponent instead of his coach. They are more than happy to take on a fight. They enjoy the fight; it engages their curiosity. To have a positive relationship with them you need to assume the role as their motivational coach. Would you have taken out a stick and told Mohammad Ali how to move his feet a little faster? I don't think so. The clever coach will not try to force this horse to perform but will understand that he is Aloof and a trait of an Aloof horse is his attachment to his job. As a good coach the trainer will need to find him a job that he likes and then help him perform it. "Help him" does not mean telling him where to put every foot.

They will confidently handle a variety of work. Hopefully, you will find a job or activity they love and can do repeatedly without too much rider influence. They love to be good at things and will play at them everyday as long as they see it as play and not work. They have opinions, and they are strong-minded about asserting their will. Most Curious horses are fun and like a lot of variety, but when it comes mixed with Dominant and Lazy, they will challenge you to keep them entertained. They make a lot of their own rules. For example:

- "Don't touch those reins. I don't DO on the bit."

- "I don't feel like leading today. There is nowhere I want to be."
- "Don't even try to teach me. I wrote the book."
- "I already said 'No.' Do I have to make that clearer?"
- "Do not tie me in the trailer. I'll have to throw a fit if you do."

The ways that these guys have to teach you about their rules are many and varied. That is where their creative "C" comes in. Some like to buck, some like to rear, some refuse to go forward, some act incredibly spooky, all in the name of outsmarting you and letting you know that they will not be told what to do. Most successful owners of the DLCA will have made some concessions along the way and come to some mutual agreements. This horse is a strong negotiator. They can be very good competitors and partners as long as you are behind them and supporting them and allowing them to perform in their own unique style. Most have their own style of HOW they are going to go. Don't mess with that too much. Turn them loose as much as possible—in the ring and out of it.

If this horse is a big 'D' for Dominant, then it is important that he lives out in a pasture setting with a herd. As with any big Dominant, it is telling us how much control he needs in his world. If you as the rider want to be in control of him for the hour that you ride, then it would be to your advantage to allow him to be out with a herd controlling others for the rest of the day. This need to control will come out somewhere, and it would be better if it was out in the pasture rather than during your ride. Their other need that will be satisfied in the herd is their Curious trait. In the herd it will involve games—nose games, herding games, bossing games, biting and kicking games. Unless you like to play those games in the hour that you ride, it is advisable that they have a lot of outside social time.

The Prize Fighter needs a bunch of "Submissives" that he can boss about. That is the role that he is trying to put you in. It will save a lot of wear and tear on you, the rider, to send him to the pasture for some quality Prize Fighter time.

Training

When training this horse, think a lot more about the carrot than the stick. If you use negative training techniques, this horse will be happy to go into the boxing ring for a round or two every day. The DLCA hates to be wrong. (Don't we all?) A problem arises here because most traditional training techniques are negatively focused meaning that the horse is left alone when he is right and receives a negative response when he is wrong. If we are telling this personality daily that he is wrong about something, he will start to resent us and the training. This creates the fight that we so frequently see with this personality.

In the positive, Prize Fighters are proud, brave and solid campaigners. Depending on the training they receive, they can either be the "Bad Boy" or the "Rock." If you can find a positive way to coach him, the bonus is that he will put you in the winner's circle.

In some barns there is pressure on trainers to keep horses progressing. The Prize Fighter will challenge the system. Remember, Prize Fighters strongly dislike being told what to do all the time. You may have bought this horse for a very hefty price tag as a youngster because he has shown so much early potential. But if he is not allowed to get on with the job, he will quit the job altogether. And when Prize Fighters quit, it is with a lot of flair—rearing, going over backward, bucking, backing and refusing to go forward. They know how to say "No." The extremely assertive, knowledgeable trainer may temporarily get them going again, but this horse will usually bide his time and come back with a new way to say to "No." The amateur owner watching this may think that this is the only way to ride this horse and try to emulate this assertive style of riding. The danger here is that someone could really get hurt. The amateur may get along with this horse, but they must give up trying to be the boss.

The person (could be a Junior) who can give this horse a lot of variety, go out and play with him, trail ride him, generally let him dictate a lot of the rules, will be able to develop a relationship with this horse. In time, the horse will start to want to go back in the ring and show off. If the rider is nervous or timid, this horse will not be affected by it as long as the relationship is strong and the horse knows and likes his job: "Sit down little lady, I can show you how it is done." They like to make deals with you: "You do this for me, and I will do that for you."

With this type of personality it is critical that trainers learn positive training techniques. Clicker training (See "Tools") could be a real asset if you are trying to retrain a Prize Fighter that has quit wanting to perform. It is really not about what you do in your training program; it is more about how you do it or where you are coming from. This horse will challenge you and make you learn to ride from a new place. Leave your ego on the shelf and find new creative ways to do things. If you do not, they will delight in making a fool out of you. Don't pick at them and tell them how to do it. If you have a need to be right, this horse has come into your life to help you get over it. Learn to enjoy them, laugh at them, reward them, cater to them, love them for who they are, and be willing to go along for the ride sometimes and see where it takes you.

Careers

Prize Fighters are one of the most competitive horse personalities. They can be found doing nearly all sports. They must do a job that they like. Then they need to be turned loose to do the job. If you find the right job for this horse, he will show up to perform every day and give you his all. Jobs that require short quick workouts will be more suited to this personality than endurance type sports. They like jobs where they can think for themselves and be left alone to get it done, like cow work, polo, barrel racing, roping or jumping. Remember that they are fighters, and if you can get them fighting FOR your cause, they will not quit and will not let you down.

Chapter 11

DLAF   The Accountant

As their name implies, these are not your "wild and crazy kinda guys." A very small percentage of the performance horse population is DLAF. They like life to be predictable, not exciting. They are honest and straightforward and expect you to be as well. Fair treatment is something that they expect—they may even demand it. Although they are a friendly horse, they are the most reserved of the Friendly. They will not be overly expressive about it. It is a quiet respect that they will show you. Solid and strong, they like life to have systems and order: "Do not change the rules— do not rush me or push me."

When we break down their personality, we find that as usual the Dominant/Lazy gives them quiet strength and determination, but the Afraid/Friendly then makes them sensitive, so that you end up with a bit of a paradox— having a dull/sensitive type of horse. This may come across in training as you have to make them do it (that is the D), but then when you do, they can overreact and suddenly appear overly responsive or flighty. This is their fear that is usually kept under wraps. They want to be the quiet strong boys, but the fear or dominance kicks in occasionally and makes them a bit conflicted.

Their dominance is expressed in a very quiet way because that is their nature. But it can be brought out quite strongly if you do not respect them and the orderly way in which they like to do things. Any time Dominant and

Lazy are together, you will have to be creative in how you motivate them to get moving. Work with their Friendly, keep them on your side, keep them safe. Keep away from their negative side, which can be sulky and passively resistant. They want to be your good, solid worker—honor them and they will be.

The Accountant, in comparing them to their closest relatives the SLAF (Wall Flowers), is different in that they are not nearly as emotional and sensitive. The solid old DLAF's are happy to plod along in the system. Our DLAF's personality does not have a big ego that needs attention like their brother the DLCF (Reluctant Rock Star). These guys do not need to be on center stage. They would probably prefer not to have all that fuss and attention. They are happy to work away in the back room, as long as you appreciate them. They are not willful like the DEAF (Wild Card) where the Energetic and Afraid create an impulsive unpredictability. This horse can be your steady, reliable partner.

Training

Actually thinking of this horse as an Accountant will really help us to work effectively with them. What does our Accountant want from us? He expects us to be honest and accountable. He wants us to have a consistent plan that we follow through on. He wants us to take care of all the small details. He wants us to have our books in order and to follow the rules. He wants to have lots of time to do his work. Leave him alone, don't pressure him. Don't dump a messy box on his desk at the last minute, or he will most likely "freak out."

So too, this horse has the capacity to freak out if the rules are broken too many times. Their Dominance will come to the forefront and you will have some "attitude" to deal with. This "attitude" will emerge as well in any sort of abusive training situation. If they are pushed too hard too many times, the gloves will be off. As mentioned earlier the fight will be expressed as passive resistance: "Make me!" If the relationship deteriorates to this point, the sad loss will be their Friendly side. These horses are not outgoing in their friendly attitude. So if something is amiss in the relationship or if they feel afraid too many times, they will shut down their Friendly; they will appear tuned out and disinterested. In this case an owner may think that they are Aloof, instead of Friendly.

Your challenge is to engage this horse in positive ways. They love reward. They do not mind repetition as long as you are pleased with their progress. Develop a training system and stick to it. Constantly changing the training program, being a guru to the latest training ideas, will not work with these horses. Honor them by always having a consistent plan before you go to the barn. They will get very attached to their program, and be very happy to go through their paces. Once they know their job and are well trained in it, they would be happy to be an amateur or children's mount. If you now have a DLAF in your life, he will inspire you to get organized, to develop your own system and to learn to stick to a plan.

Careers

This horse could be a trail horse. As a weekend pleasure mount, he would be very happy, especially if it were a sociable outing and not too strenuous. Competitive trail would likely require too much energy and show trail would be a little scary.

As a driving horse he will be your honest, strong worker. He will like the consistency of the job. He would need to be driven on a regular basis, not a once a month driving horse.

He would love the routine of chores, feeding, or working in the bush. Competitive driving would not work for them as a single as they would likely find it stressful and requiring more energy than they like to expend. But in the role of a wheeler they may work well if they have enough stamina for the distance.

The DLAF's would probably like the routine of the timed events in rodeo (such as barrel racing), because they can do the same job over and over again, and the speed is only required for a very short distance. Speed will not tend to make them crazy.

As a show hunter, the fences and courses are all very similar, and this would appeal to the Accountant. Rushing fences wouldn't be an issue. The Afraid would probably make them jump well, although they would need quite a bit of schooling to make them solid and safe.

As a Western or English Pleasure horse, they would be comfortable in rail classes as they like the group atmosphere. It would not be too strenuous physically for them, although they may not have enough ego and ring presence to make them the shining star.

They would most likely enjoy teaching people, so being a lesson horse would suit their needs fine, but only after they have learned their craft well. They would like all the attention and low stress physical demands as long as they were not in one of the salt mine type of lesson programs where school horses do ten lessons a day.

Chapter 12

DLAA   The Skeptic

If you have spent the past three years slowly and conscientiously building a trusting relationship with your horse, and in one innocent incident it has been dashed on the rocks, you probably own a DLAA. The Skeptics, as one owner named them, need to come with an operator's manual. It is not called an owner's manual because you never really own them—they are their own person/horse. In this manual the trouble shooting section would be lengthy. They all have a long list of do's and don'ts.

They have the ego of the D's without a lot of the confidence that usually accompanies it. They are skeptical of you and your methods and even their herd mates. One owner's comment on her Skeptic was that "they don't suffer fools gladly." They have BIG trust issues, and if you are prone to feeling guilty, you will feel that their problems are entirely your fault. They would concur. They prefer to have someone to blame.

In general, they take themselves very seriously. They will take their job equally seriously; they will own it. They get their confidence from their job like other Aloofs. Routine in their work is important. They like to get to the job and get it done efficiently. They have little time for a rider who is flighty, fluffy, insecure or emotional. They demand respect and will respect you equally. Most times they are very level-headed and reasonable. But we need to be aware of their Afraid. They handle Afraid like most other Dominants:

by getting angry, and that anger is usually directed at the rider.

As they are lazy and quiet most of the time it seems to come as a surprise when they suddenly can't handle something. At this point their fear needs to be honored as most can on occasion be volatile if not listened to. You need to take control and keep them protected but in a much more subtle way than with the Submissive horses who are only too happy to turn the reins over to you. Taking control of the situation does not mean forcing them to deal with the fear. It may mean walking away from it for awhile. They will overcome the fear on their own time if not pressured. Avoiding mistakes with them is critical as they are unforgiving and those years of trust can be shattered instantly.

Proceed into new territory with them with caution: because he is a cutting horse does not mean he can automatically become a penning horse, because he is a good hunter does not mean he will be a good jumper. They will tell you if they like their job or not—believe them. It will be in your best interest.

Training

Trust will be the ongoing issue with the Skeptic. You will need to prove to them again and again that you are trustworthy, that you are safe, dependable, and predictable. They have dignity and want to be respected. Only when they feel that respect is mutual will they begin working with you instead of against you.

You will need to fine-tune your listening skills to understand what they are trying to say. They appear quiet, reserved, almost stoic at times and so they can easily be misread. Do not expect them to be engaging, expressive and outgoing. You will learn to read the subtle changes and make adjustments to your program. You need to follow a structured program that makes sense to them. If they start to get frustrated from not understanding and the trainer keeps on pushing, then the dominant explosive side will be ignited. They need time and repetition to learn.

They want to be quiet good boys, but they do get afraid sometimes. Then they need that fair and firm partner to help them through it. They want to know what the rules are well in advance and want to know they will not change. They will also make a few of their own. Once they are on your side, they see you as a partner so you can allow them quite a bit of latitude in HOW they do something. Some days you help them; some days they help you.

They do not look for mischief, for challenges, for accolades. They are happy to do the same job day in and day out, as long as they like it. What would be terribly boring to others is fine with them. Change (whether it is tack, bit, rider, trails, job, trailer) must be approached carefully and with a systematic plan, always listening for feedback and not pushing beyond their comfort level. They need time to process new information. Get a little and then leave them alone.

Careers

If you have a job that you need help with, then this is your horse. As with other Aloof horses it is important for them to get a job early and understand what it is. The Skeptic is not a "Jack of all trades." Their job can be simple. It does not need to be a competitive career. They would be happy as a trail horse, a ranch horse, a hunt horse, a rope horse—any of these, just pick one. Once they understand their job, they do not need constant riding or schooling. What you had last month is what you will get this month. They like consistency in their life, in their job and in you.

Chapter 13

SECF   The Goddess

If a Goddess horse has found his way into your barn, you are lucky. If you are wise as well, you will not let him leave. Most SECF's do not change hands often as they work their way into your heart and stay. You should feel honored to be one of their subjects. They will give back as much as they receive. They are loved and appreciated everywhere, including in the pasture. The Bosses will protect them, and the other Submissives will try to get as close as possible. They are happy to meet you at the gate and play at whatever you are doing. Usually quite vocal, this horse will be the one nickering to you when you get out of your car or open your front door.

SECF's have feminine looks as well as characteristics. They are emotional and sensitive and yet still confident. They are wonderfully sensible and safe. They aren't inclined to get into trouble with you or with their environment like some of the other C's. Everything about their demeanor denotes expression—they are talkative, have expressive eyes and ears, active movement, love to touch you, love to show off, act sassy but never in a dominant way, just enough to endear them to you more. If you want a horse to love on, then this is your baby. They like to be clean, pretty, pampered, blanketed, groomed, and fussed over in any fashion.

An older thoroughbred breeding stallion that we had at the ranch was a Goddess. (I am sure he would not have approved of that name!) Like all Goddesses, he was gentle and kind and very chatty. He was used to pasture breeding and watching him with his mares was a delight. They let him pretend he was boss. One year a small quarter horse mare decided that he should be all hers (she was a Prize Fighter) and after she was bred refused to let him breed any other mares. She would march over and promptly tell him to "get off." He would comply. This is just another example of how loved the Goddess is whether in the herd or in your barn.

Beware though. If they are uncomfortable, unhappy or sore, they can be very expressive with a cranky pinning of the ears and a swish of the tail! It pays to listen. They are trying to tell you something.

For the Goddess the relationship is paramount. It is what they love, and they would love to engage in long conversations about it if they could. They trust you, and you can trust them. They want to be your partner, and they need you to be listening. If they feel unappreciated, they can spiral downhill into a puddle of worry and insecurity. These are the traits of Submissive and Friendly together. Like other C's they can get bored easily, so you do need an interactive, engaging relationship. They will want a lot of variety in the things that you do together. Your relationship will be strengthened when the Goddess's need to be doing things, especially with you, is met.

Like any of the Energy/Curious horses they can have scattered energy at times that is hard to get focused on the task at hand. In their initial training, you may feel that they have "fluff for brains" and you might describe them as the "blond" of the barn. Their energy can be bouncing off the walls. They can be oversensitive, and if you get them upset, it takes them a long time to settle them back down again.

Some days it is best to walk away and begin again tomorrow. The next day they will be back on your page and trying to please. The Friendly says they love to please and will keep trying and trying in their job. This can make them worriers if they do not understand and are not feeling honored. If they are not being listened to and appreciated, they will usually internalize their stress and can develop physical problems, especially back problems. As their rider, your job will be to help them learn to focus and keep their energies more in balance.

It is difficult for the Goddess to change owners. Not only do we get very attached to these horses, but they to us as well. They show obvious signs of depression when they are sold. It may take them quite a while to adjust to a new owner. They love new situations but like to keep their people the same. At any time, the Goddess dislikes being alone, but they are especially vulnerable in this situation. What can you do to help? The SECF needs to know you are there for him, so if the new owners can understand his personality they will know that they need to pay him a lot of extra special attention when they first get him. Keep the work demands low and the love and attention high. This horse will suffer if left on their own without attention. They love being in a herd situation with all the social intricacies.

Training

Training the Goddess is a pleasure and does not require you to have numerous horse training degrees. Unlike the Dominants, they are quite happy to accept your suggestions on how something should be done. The greatest challenge will be keeping the foundation lessons interesting enough. The SECF will be anxious to get on to the higher learning. Give them a lot of variety and take them to a lot of new places. They will love to travel and experience new things. They like a communicative rider who is as enthusiastic as them.

If they have a high E, it may make it hard for them to slow down and learn in the beginning. They will be anticipating and offering things that you are not asking for. Positive reinforcement is the key as they will thrive in that type of training program. As they are very engaged and emotional in everything they do they can have their days or times where you will have to quietly sit in the middle and just allow some of the energy to dissipate. They are not trying to take over like the D's, so a rider does not have to come on strong in response. They may just need a little help learning how to release so much emotion. If training is starting to get heated up, just relax and go for a ride out; tomorrow they will be back on track and eager to please.

The Submissive trait of the Goddess tells us that there will be times that we will need to be there for them every step of the way. If they are learning something new or in a fearful situation, they will want to turn over the command to you. They will need you to tell them where to put every foot. The 'leg to hand' type of ride will be comforting to them in this situation, but they do not need it every day.

This horse comes into our life to help us learn about relationships and bonding—they are in it FOR the relationship.

Careers

You will find the SECF performing in all horse sports. They may not be on the top of the podium as often as the DECF's (Rock Stars), but every step of the way has been a pleasure. Whatever your sport, this horse is happy to do it. They are the "keeners." They are not attached to the job. They are working to please you. In competitive fields they are your high point, super horse, all round contenders. Your challenge will be to not get stuck exclusively in one sport. This horse will encourage you to broaden your horizons and go play in new fields.

Chapter 14

SECA   The Worker Bee

If, out in your herd, there is a rather non-descript "good" horse that doesn't draw or need a lot of attention, chances are, he is an SECA. The Worker Bee doesn't take up a lot space or time and is just fine to float along on the edge of life waiting for his next assignment. He is compliant and willing to do a variety of things without needing a lot of approval or ego stroking. Save your kudos. He is happy to be the Worker Bee as long as you have learned to be the queen bee.

To the Worker Bee the job is all important. They do not have a lot of time for fluffy relationship stuff like the SECF (Goddess). Give them jobs that are interesting and challenging and be there to help them accomplish it. They do not fly solo! They have a soft ego so do not need a fancy career, but they do need a confident rider that has a clear vision of what needs to be accomplished. They are matter of fact, easy to motivate, with energy and a strong work ethic. All they need are guidelines to follow. If not given guidelines, they can worry and be insecure.

Although Aloof and content to spend time slightly away from the herd, the Curious part of their personality makes Worker Bees quite playful with their herd mates. Their Submissive side makes them need to be with someone who is in control whether in the herd or on the job. They do not need constant input like the SEAF's (People Pleasers), but they do need direction. They are not aggressive or mean with people or other horses. On the job, they will keep trying to please, be quite forgiving, and even permit mistakes. They can therefore recover from an accident or wreck with minimal emotional damage as long as the next time you are there for them and tell them what to do. They do not hold grudges. They will step right back up to the plate and be willing to listen again. They are just anxious to get back on the job. Be the leader for this horse, and he will perform a solid job.

Training

SECA's are easy to train as long as the trainer has a concise training program. Show this horse what the job is early on, and he will be a willing participant. Yes, still appreciate them but do not mollycoddle them. Again, they are serious workers. Because they are not working the Friendly, they are not above taking advantage of a rider with soft boundaries and can become quite insecure without that solid frame of reference that they rely upon. They are happy to play by the rules, so make sure your rules are well-defined. In good hands they come across deceivingly confident, so be aware if you are looking at buying one that you can provide the same kind of firm guidelines.

The Dominant horses scoff at a lot of our ground games. But for the Submissives they are a valuable asset to your training program. At times, the Worker Bee may need some ground work to wear off some of that energy or to help you initially establish dominance. Round penning (See "Tools") will work well to help them see that you are the leader and that they are safe with you. Turning them loose and sending them away will help them understand that they can find their safety with you. On the opposite end of the scale, if they are an overly needy type of SECA, then line driving would be a better ground exercise as it shows them that you can still be there for them even when they are away from you. They need to work independent of you, but still be listening. Lunging may not work as well because with their high energy they may just run in circles getting fitter and fitter. You may have to return to the dominant leading exercise (see "Tools") frequently just to remind them to keep their energy in check and to turn the leadership over to you.

This horse will gain confidence being sent forward, unlike the SEAF (People Pleaser) or the SEAA (Perfectionist) who has to walk before he can run. The Curious trait is what gives them confidence, and the Energetic trait along with attachment to job makes them like to get out and work things through, not sit around and talk about it. The timid rider who wants to make sure everything is perfect before proceeding will have a harder time with this horse because this horse is looking for leadership. The sending forward tells them that a confident captain is on board.

If you want a companion pleasure horse that you can play with and love on, this horse may not be the best match for you. They will be bored, have far too much energy and will likely try to take advantage of your kindness. If you have a sport or job that requires a hard worker this personality will fit in beautifully as long as you carry your own confidence. They will have a "bring it on" attitude for new things—just be there for them. As they are Submissive and Energetic, this automatically predisposes them to sensitivity. They are eager to please, so you do not need to come on as a "10." As long as they are confident that you are above them in the pecking order, they will be happy to be your Worker Bee.

Careers

SECA's will be successful at a wide variety of jobs. With a confident rider they can handle speed and high energy roles such as polo, jumping, barrels, eventing, cow work, endurance riding. They are not your teachers—your school masters. When they do not find leadership, they can spiral down into insecurities. In later years, they will be fine for the beginner, as long as they know and like their job.

Chapter 15

SEAF   The People Pleaser

"Am I doing a good job?"

"Are you happy with me?"

"Do you still like me?"

SEAF's have a million questions and they over-analyze everything. Never give them your cell phone—they will be calling every ten minutes! Insecurities abound in their lives. They are constantly trying to fit in and be liked. They are sometimes described as delightfully sensitive; at other times as incredibly needy and uncertain. You may have rescued one that you felt was being misunderstood. The challenge now is in your court to try and figure out what this horse needs to be able to relax and enjoy life.

Easy to love! They are touchy, cuddly, expressive, cute, loveable, and smart. They try so hard but worry so much. You want to wrap them up, take them home and keep them safe. Safety should be your main priority if you want to work successfully with this type. They need to be kept safe. They are afraid of many things in their world. Because they are Submissive and Friendly, a lot of their fear is rider directed. They are trying so hard to please, that it comes across as not listening because they are over-responding and over-reacting.

Add Energy to this personality and it is like adding fuel to the fire. They are spinning their wheels and revving off in six directions. They need to be kept in a small box so that they know exactly what to do and where to put their feet. Routine is critical for them. They find any change stressful, whether it is new places, new jobs, new owners, or new pasture mates. The less Submissive types will externally express this emotion through motion, while the more Submissive ones will internalize their feelings and be the ones that colic easily or develop ulcers. Your emotions as well as theirs need to be managed carefully. If you get emotional, they will get emotional.

They will appear psychic in the way they can pick up on how you are feeling today. If they are pushed into overload, they can have explosive outbursts. Listening to them and calmly and quietly returning to a lesson that they know well may save the day.

SEAF's need constant input and assurance that they are doing everything right. The relationship is much more important to them than the job. Their worries are not about the job or external environment nearly as much as how you feel about them. Like the DEAF's (Wild Cards), they would be happy to do the same circle for eight years as long as it made you happy. They do not need a lot of variety and exciting challenges. They are emotional, expressive and fairly feminine, similar to the SECF's (Goddess), but lacking some of that personality's confidence and grace. It is hard to look graceful when sweating and worrying.

A somewhat conflicting characteristic that shows up occasionally (in small herd situations) is the desire to be bossy and controlling even though they are Submissive. They may repeatedly try to push the herd boss away from his food even though they never succeed. Owners watching this may be confused and think that they have a Dominant horse making them a DEAF or Wild Card. Reading the characteristics of that personality would soon reassure them that they do in fact own a Submissive horse. This horse will never challenge and fight with them like a Wild Card. But why the bossiness? Perhaps they feel that their world is out of control and are struggling to put some order in it.

They need you to have a quiet, consistent program and be understanding and fair with them. Keep your expectations low. They are insecure, so they need a confident, relaxed rider on whom they can rely. If their rider gets nervous, tight or tense, they will respond likewise by getting nervous, tight and tense. Help them to manage their emotions because they can't. If left without input, before long, their busy mind will send them rushing off in some direction that will take their rider totally by surprise. In the hands of a relaxed confident horseperson, this horse will not put a foot out of place because that rider will be telling them exactly where to put every foot. In spite of their complexities, People Pleasers are loved and appreciated companions by most of their owners.

Training

Enroll this horse in the three-year training program. They will need all the time you can spend with them and more. New things must be introduced slowly and repeated frequently until you are both probably a little bored. At this point the SEAF will finally understand that he is in fact doing the right thing and start to relax and consequently develop some confidence.

This horse is easy to make mistakes with as they can get in over their heads quickly. Because they are trying so hard, riders think that they have got it and proceed on to more advanced work before they are ready and eventually the horse derails. They are dealing with fear and energy, so it is your job to slow it all down until they understand. This horse must walk before he runs. He must understand his training very well at the walk, before proceeding up through the other paces.

Some riders will think that they can lunge or exercise this horse to get him to quiet down. As the speed increases, the internal chatter increases until nothing is making any sense and you both feel frustrated and upset. That is why the canter can take a long time to develop in this personality. The wind in their ears is whispering many things. But as they learn to allow you to control them, you can start to slow it all down and make it work for them.

Ground games are great for these horses as it gives them a place to build the relationship and trust, which is really what they are looking for. They need the relationship. They need to be listened to. Any erratic expectations in your program will lead to erratic behavior on their part. They do not hold grudges, but are easily damaged emotionally.

A trainer must never lose his cool with this horse. The damage may be irreparable. This horse doesn't just develop issues from abuse. They develop full blown phobias and disorders. The best ground exercises to build a solid foundation would be ground driving or long lining. With round pen or lunging, their energy makes it hard for them to slow down and understand the exercise. They will worry if we are always sending them away. They need to know that we are constantly there for them.

Owners have found this horse slow to mature. Perhaps we are inclined to baby them because they are so uncertain and insecure, which is maybe why we frequently rescue them. But we must understand that no amount of love is going to make them feel safe. We need to take their hand and guide them through life. This is why the confident rider who can tell the People Pleaser where to place every foot has success with this type. And when the rider does it in a quiet way that is constantly reassuring this horse that he is doing everything right, the SEAF will blossom and shine.

However, just because they shine in the hands of one person, does not mean they can with another. Without the same confident ride, they could easily fall apart even though they appear to know their job. Remember they are Friendly, not Aloof, so they do not attach to their job. They are attached to you. They can become a one-man horse.

An SEAF show jumper I have watched over the years has excelled in this type of quiet, consistent program. Her name is Rayana, and her rider has been there for her every step of the way. He is a pro who is able to slow her world down and tell her exactly what to do and when. In return, she turns her entire trust over to him. They competed in the Puissance event at Spruce Meadows one year. This is a competitive event in which the horse and rider are required to jump a solid wall and are eliminated if they knock down any of it. The wall is built higher each round and the last remaining horse/rider pair is the winner. You would not normally think that this personality could possibly do that event. For her to jump such a large and imposing obstacle was credit to the type of ride she received. Others watching were not nearly as in awe as I was because I knew her personality—I knew she was doing this feat entirely to please him. He gave her the ideal ride. In the competition they have one or two smaller jumps to warm up and then down to the big wall. Each time after jumping the smaller fence, her rider stopped her and patted her, letting her know what a good job she was doing, then would pick up a canter and ride on down to the big wall. She gave him her all. They finished by jumping 6'1". He retired from the competition at that point, knowing that she had done her best for him. Who knew a pat could mean so much? It does to this personality.

Careers

The People Pleaser horse is not actually looking for a serious job. He is happy being your companion at work or otherwise as long as you are appreciating him for his part. They do not like to be left on their own, so the job must be one that you can help them with. They are not your once-a-week pleasure horses as they need a lot of riding, but trail riding will appeal to them as it is relatively low stress.

They could make a lovely hunter as they usually have a very cute jump because they are a bit afraid, but the energy is sometimes too much for hunters. They would like the repetition as long as you dictate the ride. Jumpers might have too much variety and speed, unless you were the type of rider that could really slow it all down for them. They will jump clean but may have trouble when you add speed. They would probably like dressage as they would like you telling them where to put every foot as long as you proceed through the levels slowly and do not put too much pressure on them. They would enjoy competitive trail, as they would have all the energy you need, and they would love all the miles and time that you spend with them in that type of sport. The People Pleaser does not care too much what you do, just as long as you care.

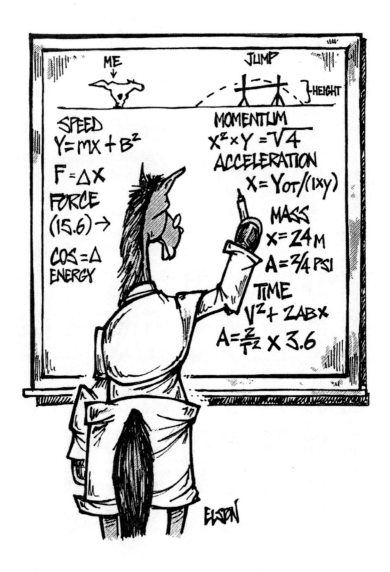

Chapter 16

SEAA   The Perfectionist

In a perfect world this horse would turn out perfectly. Ideally they would be born to a confident, caring mother. Their first interaction with people would be imprinting to help them cope with all that life is going to throw at them. They would be handled regularly as babies, weanlings and yearlings. Their education would have a solid base that is built on trust. Their training would be started when they are young and malleable; they would be ridden regularly; they would be given tools to help them remain in control rather than reacting; they would be treated as an individual and not compared with the other youngsters in the program; their trainers would be experienced, quiet, confident; and their herd would remain constant without new horses coming and going on a regular basis. They would find a job that they attach to at an early age, that they can do well and that brings them satisfaction and a sense of confidence.

This would be the success story for the Perfectionist. Sadly, this is rarely the case for young horses. And so, where other personalities can cope and learn on the fly from various different trainers with different expectations and find a place to fit in at different barns and in new pastures, the Perfectionist gets frustrated and angry and afraid in changing situations. They can decide that they would rather not participate at all. Running away can become their evasion of choice whether out in the field or with you riding them. If we find one in our barn, perhaps we can arm ourselves with enough knowledge to be able to fill in a lot of the missing pieces and still end up with our perfect horse.

In the negative they may be nervous, suspicious, high strung, worried, fearful, or anxious. Their insecurities abound. They appear to be timid, frightened, even abused. You may have seen them in someone else's hands and wanted to save them. Now what do you do with them? Their emotional coping mechanisms are limited. You may pour your heart and soul into them without a lot of warmth coming back. The reason for this is their Aloof. They may eventually settle and become easier to catch and a little happier and secure in their environment.

But if they have been damaged, the Energetic/Afraid/Aloof says that their evasion of choice is running away from everything. They can be calculating, smart and unforgiving, even holding grudges if offended. They wear their "issues" like badges. The negative ones have been described in such unsavory terms as "paranoid" or "psycho." They have been voted "most likely to leave the relationship," because that is often the only solution that they see available and they have an unlimited amount of energy with which to do it.

Even in the herd, they do not seem to be socially well-adjusted. They do not make friends easily and appear at times to be caught in a conflict of being Afraid and therefore needing the herd while at the same time wanting to be Aloof and alone. They resent their dependence on the herd and on you.

We have an old horse in our herd named Sinalta. He and his owner have done nothing for fifteen years — "irreconcilable differences." At the last attempt at catching, Sin ran for 6 hours. He won. His owner gave up. Now as a senior, given cookies every time we go out to the herd, he appears sociable to us, as he makes his way over for his cookie. His years of running away are over. But still we see how aloof and indifferent he is with the herd. Whenever we are doing herd check, it always requires extra time to find Sin. He will be off by himself, still within sight of the herd, but quite separate. When they come into the corral, he will wait outside. When they leave, he will then come in for a drink. I would have described him as the Lone Wolf (SLAA), but his high energy makes him quite different from that personality and once we started doing personality testing we realized that he was a Perfectionist. He did not unfortunately receive that ideal upbringing. He was started late, trained by an inexperienced rider, ridden inconsistently, and thrown into a variety of jobs and sports. His reaction to life and people was to run away, and eventually his owner gave up on him. With our understanding of what this personality needs we have now gained his trust and we will have to be content with that for this horse.

If you love challenges and a project, then this horse is the one for you. If you have raised a youngster and have concluded that he is an SEAA, then you have the chance to put him in the right kind of program so that he can become the Perfectionist that he would really love to be.

In the positive, this horse will want to listen to you and want your support and encouragement with the job. It will be about the job, and they will have ample energy to throw at it. This horse does not tire. He will be happy to repeat patterns and school frequently. As long as you are there for him in the performance, they will give you 120 percent. They like to be good at what they do and will have the work ethic to make it so.

Training

As with all Submissive horses, SEAA's will need you to tell them what to do. How you do that will determine if they can function successfully in their world! You need to prove to them again and again that you will keep them safe and not expect more of them than what they can deliver. They need a linear program with very few deviations or distractions. Their progress may be slow, with many safety circles or miles on the trail. With this horse you walk in a circle until he can relax. Once the walk is established, then you move up through the paces. As you venture out of the safety circle, if he becomes upset, you return to it and back to where they can find a quiet place to be. They can be impatient, but you must never be. As a rider you will need to be quiet and not bombard them with too much information. You will need to be confident in what you present to them as they will pick up every slight shift of emotion or doubt.

As one trainer who worked with a Perfectionist commented, "You need to put a blanket over them and cuddle them." Now that is a safety net! A job that requires them to be constantly learning and challenged will leave them in constant anxiety. They are Perfectionists, so they need to do well at whatever they are learning. In the beginning stages this can be difficult. That is where the repetition comes in: they need to not just understand a piece of the training program but to have it repeated often enough that they are excellent at it, even if it is something simple like a leg yield.

A solid successful base is critical, so spending the time to build that is of the utmost importance. This is what is difficult in so many professional barns because clients want to see results, and if the trainer is still working on ground work three months into the training, they think there is something wrong. It is probably exactly what this horse needs. They cannot be trained on the same program as the other colts in the barn. Triple your time and then be patient. As early as possible, get them to a place where they have a job and are excellent at it.

The most successful SEAA's are the ones that are not extreme in any personality trait. The most difficult horses are those whose Energetic and Afraid traits are off the chart. These horses are running from life most of the time. The Submissive trait can be extreme as long as the rider is quite competent and can quietly be running the show.

This horse will need to be protected by the rider and should be able to listen and perform if they are competing or working at something they like. They will have endless energy to put into your sport. If you are dominant, bold, and confident with a nurturing side, you could have a successful partnership with this horse. If the romantic notion of having a one-man horse appeals to you, this horse could be the one for you.

Careers

Like some of us, perhaps it would appear the Perfectionist has been born a century too late. Can you imagine what a great stage coach horse or pony express horse the Perfectionist would make? He could run for miles and not have to think. On a great day, there could be a hold up or an ambush and then the driver would be yelling and actually asking him to go faster instead of holding him in. Bonus!

Perhaps they would like to be the modern-day chuckwagon horse, but who would want the job of holding them at the barrel before the race or initially teaching them to drive. As a race horse, they would be very hard to rate and navigate through traffic. The first quarter might be at a dazzling speed but then it may drastically fall off. The gate schooling would also be very scary. Steeple chase might be fast and sporting enough for them.

It is doubtful if this horse would perform well in any arena sport, unless they have that ideal, perfect upbringing.

Distance riding? Now that might be perfect for them. It would definitely have to be endurance racing, not competitive trail riding. They would hate all the waiting and rating that is required in competitive trail. The first five miles of the endurance race might be a little hairy, but then they would probably settle down and be a delight. A problem with competitive distance horses is "buddying up" with another horse, whinnying and worrying constantly about where that other horse is while on the trail or at the vet checks. This would not be problem for the SEAA as they are not overly social. They most likely would enjoy the solitary miles that you put in together in training for the event as well. You would be there for them but not be giving them too much stimulation, exactly what they need to feel safe. This may be your Tevis Cup horse!

Chapter 17

SLCF   The Steady Eddy

If your world has been rocked (in a negative way) by a horse, then the next horse you need to get on is the SLCF. The Steady Eddy will instill confidence and be the perfect horse for making you feel safe, capable and secure. They are ideal for the amateur adult learning to ride because they are forgiving and accepting of mistakes. This horse is not waiting for the opportunity to take advantage of you. Even as young horses or when relatively green, they will still try to figure out what you want and strive to comply. Children or seniors are usually safe if matched with this personality type.

Most owners form deep and lasting relationships with the Steady Eddy. They are friendly and a pleasure to be around. Some riders wanting excitement and challenge may find them a bit boring due to their low energy level. But for the person who has a soft personality and who does not like constantly having to be the boss or leader, this horse will be a delight, going along for the ride without a lot of question. They therefore make the ideal pleasure mount. They do not require a lot of exercise. In fact, they prefer minimal activity, so they can be left in the field for weeks and still be enjoyable when you bring them out to do something. They do not NEED to have a job, they are quite happy to "tootle."

If you need a horse to teach you a new sport or skill, this horse is ideal because he will allow you to make mistakes.

These horses will try anything for you and will positively glow from compliments and approval. Your relationship with them is much more important than what they do, so they are happy to try any sport that makes you happy. Even if not aptly suited for it, they still give their best trying to please you. They like learning new things as long as you acknowledge their effort. Like the SECF's (Goddesses), they are expressive and want to be listened to and understood. Even as young horses, they seem amazingly able to handle a variety of situations with ease.

Most Submissives require a rider to be confident and be ready to take control of any situation, but the Steady Eddies are Lazy and prefer to think things through rather than put a lot of energy into a reaction. The Lazy trait here is a positive attribute, but it can, in this horse, leave riders feeling fairly challenged if they want to progress and compete or ride at a higher level. They do not carry their own motivation for their sports. They really could not care less about what sport you are doing. They are there for you.

If pushed too much, they can develop nervous problems and become worriers. Most people realize where they are best suited and allow them to shine in their own way. They are not usually found at the top of the podium, but they may have taught many riders who eventually get there. Their low key ego is quite content with that. They can be your workers who plod along in the same job for years, like a dude string or trail horse. They will be safe and dependable and hopefully have riders who appreciate them for what they do.

Training

The Steady Eddy is happy in any training program. He does not need one specifically designed for him. He can fit in. He will be your easy colt in the barn, not necessarily the star but certainly not the challenge either. For someone wanting to try starting their own horse for the first time, this colt would be the ideal choice. He will try to figure out what you want and forgive any ineptness. They are happy to repeat things or have new things thrown at them. Your program does not need to be foolproof. They are adaptable, but if pushed too far too fast they can develop nervous behaviors common in Submissive horses like cribbing or weaving. This is more prevalent in the high energy group. Most trainers realize quickly that Steady Eddies are not superstars so find them homes with junior or amateur riders where they can thrive.

Careers

The perfect pleasure horse! Any low key energy job that pleases you is going to be okay with them. They can be found in the lower levels of most sports. They will be the low level competitor that you see in the show ring year after year putting in solid good rounds with a new rider every year or two. If their jumping form is good, they can do well at hunter although they may never have the super star eye appeal to excel at higher levels. Safe, solid, dependable— that's how they will do your job.

Chapter 18

SLCA   The Solo Artist

Your friends marvel at what a delightfully quiet horse you have. You forget to appreciate this quality because you are spending more time and energy trying to get this horse to do a job than it would take to do the job yourself. You own a "slacker," or, as this personality type is called, a Solo Artist. These horses need to be supervised every inch of the way; if you let up for a moment, the work ceases. They are always looking for the easy way out, just trying to get by. They do just enough to avoid getting into BIG trouble. This horse could easily be your stereotypical government employee—they won't mess up enough to be fired but their resume will never say "exceeding expectations" either. They would take delight in having you fill out fifteen forms of irrelevant information. They are just sliding along each month from "haycheque to haycheque."

SLCA's do not have their own motivation. If you want them to work, then you will need to be there to make it happen. They are not your "pick me, pick me" kind of keeners. They hang back hoping someone else will sign up for the job first. As they are Submissive, you will not have to be extremely tough or strong in your training methods to get this horse to buckle down. This horse's modus operandi for getting out of something is passive resistance. This is how they seem to engage their Curiosity: "How far can I push an issue?" or "How many small annoying things can I do before they really lose it?"

And if you do lose it on occasion, they will look at you like, "What is with you today—a little testy aren't we?" Horse trainers have always told us not to personalize our horses' behavior. After all, "He is just being a horse." But this horse makes you question that. "Why is this nice little horse that seems so quiet and accepting the one that can push my buttons?" Perhaps their "C" is for Creative, creative ways to make you work harder. You are not allowed to be a passenger on this horse. You must be constantly supervising. They are not hard to catch as running away would require too much energy, but they are not likely to come to you either. They wait. They enjoy seeing you work.

People will describe them as bombproof. They love exploring new places, traveling and learning new jobs as long as it is kept fun and not stressful. This is not a Submissive horse that needs to be kept in a box. They are not afraid of much, but they can take a singular odd thing and be unrealistic about their fear of it. With one Solo Artist it was birds; another, pink poles; another, jackets; another, ditches—anything else they were not affected by. The SLCA will walk up to and touch, almost defiantly, things that would frighten most horses. But when you are riding them you must always be aware of "their thing."

Birds—what horse is afraid of birds? And we do not mean big horse-eating birds. No, blackbirds, ducks, crows, even chickens would send him into a frenzy—horribly frightening creatures. Spike is a compact little quarter horse, who is lazy and quiet, who you have to push a little just to keep moving. I am idling along out on a trail ride, very relaxed and enjoying the day, when whamo! A blackbird flies out of a crop and Spike is making a move sideways that would awe his cutting horse dad. I'm grabbing any piece of leather that I am still in contact with. We continue on our trail ride ever watchful for BIRDS! How crazy is this? He appears to enjoy my twitches when a bird flutters in the woods. He never spooks when I spook. I voted him "horse most likely to pull your groin."

This went on for years until I was introduced to clicker training. I thought I would give this a try to help solve the bird issue, which he has had since he was a two year-old. Armed with a pocket of cookies, we head out in search of birds. I decide on ducks because I know where they can usually be found. We amble along beside the pond and sure enough one flies up and I get my spook. In the middle of it, I grab leather and I "cluck." He stops and whirls his head around to get his cookie. Now some people might think that I am rewarding unwanted behavior. Is this how clicker training works? He spooks; I give him a cookie. Well, I certainly had tried the negative training for this (spurring or smacking him). All that seemed to get us was him being ever more vigilant for THE BIRDS! I wanted him to relate the cookies to the birds—all good stuff. So we carry on our ride and sure enough a duck flies up again and not a flinch—well actually, there was one from me after years of conditioning. Spike's ears are back on me checking to see if there is a cookie forthcoming. "Cluck!" Of course there is. And I rejoice because this is so much better than a pulled groin!

Training

The SLCA's are easy to train. They are quiet and will think things through rather than react. They are not overly sensitive, so they can listen to what is being asked of them. They do not like to stand out or be in trouble, so they will float along as one of the easy colts in the barn. The challenge will start to emerge as you want to really get them engaged in the training, and if you start to push, more of their passive resistance will emerge.

Here is where some psychology will come in handy. They are bored with the rider that wants to show them where to put every step and is stuck in a routine and a program. They want to live OUTside the box. They are not motivated like the Friendly horse, by pleasing you. The Solo Artist (or slacker) needs a paycheque—some form of motivation. Traditional pressure release training is difficult with this horse because they DO think things through enough to know just how little they can do to not be in trouble. No spectacular performances have been achieved this way. Positive motivation like Clicker Training (see "Tools") will work very well on this type of horse as it challenges their active minds to get their feet active. It allows you a way to give them many little paycheques. It allows you a way to motivate forward.

Slow to go and quick to quit describes the SLCA. "Whoa" may be their favorite word. It will work well as a reward in your program, after the forward issue has been addressed. Oh, and while you're at it, don't repeat the activity over and over again. You may only get three or four practice runs before they are ready to move on to something else.

As with all the Aloof horses, the job is important to them. The most important part is what they think of it. Listen to them and help them find jobs they like as they believe their agenda is much more important than yours. Once they learn a job and like it, they can be left to it, much more like a Dominant than a Submissive. Routine will put these horses to sleep, so keep a lot of variety in their weekly schedule. A different job every day would be fine with them. Short, fast, exciting jobs are great as they do not get overly revved and the excitement helps create some energy.

Careers

Any work that requires short quick workouts will suit this type. Rodeo, jumping, gymkana, hunter, or barrels — any of these would be suitable. They make the ideal all round horse or the ideal pleasure horse if you like doing a variety of things. If they show an interest in something, you may want to do their sport instead of constantly trying to get them to do yours. If they have a job they like, they will be quiet and work well for a novice or junior, but as a children's mount be aware they may constantly be trying to outsmart them.

Chapter 19

SLAF   The Wall Flower

The SLAF's are the Wall Flowers waiting on the sidelines for life to come to them. From my experience, this unique personality makes up a small percentage of the horse population. They are sweet and soft, insecure and sensitive, quiet and tentative, love to be touched and love to please you. One owner described her Wall Flower as "sticky friendly." Another described this personality as "peeking out at life." Not a lot of ego needing to be satisfied here.

Most SF's (Submissive and Friendly) have a strong desire to please you, but this personality does not have the energy and outward expression of the other ones. It is sometimes hard to know how they are feeling. They have the Afraid trait in them, but it runs so silently and they are so quiet that it is deceiving. This horse is not snorting and blowing or whirling and spinning. At times, they seem stuck in their tracks, not wanting to do the wrong thing, almost afraid to express how they feel. They look to you for safety and security. They will be wary and "sticky" in almost all new situations. Bravery is not one of their characteristics. Confidence and trust will have to be built up slowly and gradually. They have a low tolerance for anything new. This horse does not live large. He is quite happy to live in a small box. They do not need fanfare and center stage. A life fulfilled for this horse could be standing in the paddock being petted.

Most often seen as quiet and nice, they can be easily misread. As they are lazy, they do not tell us something is bothering them until it is really bothering them. If there is too much pressure at the wrong time, they can come undone. Learning to listen to their subtle signs of stress will make an artful trainer out of you.

With one of the Wall Flowers I know, her only sign that she was getting stressed was her respiration going up—no prancing or dancing or external signs. Because they are not showing obvious signs of concern, it is easy to push them into situations that are too much for them to handle and then have them blow up.

They are soft and sweet and want us to love them. Like the SEAF's (People Pleasers) they try so hard to please you that it is easy for them to get in over their heads. They want to be the easy going type, but sometimes they can't handle it. One owner said, "They feel real bad when they buck you off."

Our Wall Flowers are not only needy with us, but also worry about their pasture mates. They become bonded easily to others and have trouble being by themselves. A solid weaning program is a must with this type or the quiet timid one can suddenly become a hysterical, screaming menace. Even as a mature horse, separation anxiety can be problematic especially if you are an acreage owner. The pretty little Wall Flower may no longer be a pleasure. It will take slow consistent steps to help them overcome this issue.

Training

Slow and steady wins the race here. Rushing this horse with his learning can take you ten steps backwards. They develop trust in you by you allowing them to learn at their pace. Proceed to the next step in training with caution.

It is imperative that this horse knows that you are the leader. The challenge here is showing them you are the boss without making them afraid. They are soft and sensitive. They do not need to be handled roughly in any way to understand that you are the boss. This needs to be established initially by ground work, doing dominant leading exercises, then quiet round pen work (see "Tools") or long line driving. This horse would love programs like Lyons or Parelli as the repetition would be ideal and they would lap up all the "friendly" games.

The quiet firm trainer should not have a problem here, no matter what program they use. They will establish a solid foundation, making sure each step can be done consistently and softly before going on to the next step. They will make sure that the horse understands everything in their small playground before venturing out into bigger fields. They will listen for those respirations going up and know that they need to retreat back into safer territory and build more emotional stability. These horses want to be your friend, want to please you, but you do need to give them guidelines so that they feel safe.

Any horses with the AF (Afraid and Friendly) traits need to have a leader because they do not carry a lot of their own confidence. They need constant reassurance that they are doing the right thing. However, one interesting thing to note is the following: it would appear these horses practice their lessons out in the field. They have such a high desire to please that if you get just a hint of the right movement in your ride and you quit on it, they will come in the next time and have it. Or this may be the Lazy factor, which means they need to be allowed to think things through on their own when things are quiet. They have trouble thinking if the pressure is on.

Wall Flowers can not be turned loose to do the job. They want details and assistance on how it should be done every step of the way. They would be list makers. The Submissive factor makes this even more critical. Remember that the DAF (Dominant, Afraid and Friendly as in Wild Card or Accountant) will say, "If you are my friend, then I must be in control", because they are the bossy types. But the Submissive with these same traits (as in the People Pleaser and Wall Flower) will say, "If you are my friend, then who is in control?" Love them up on the ground, spend lots of time with them without asking much of them, but make sure they know you are the leader and will take control of any situation that arises when you are riding them.

Some inexperienced riders will try to reassure this personality type when something scares them with soft words or pats. They are trying to appeal to their friendly side, but this will send the SLAF into panic or paralysis. What this type needs in a frightening situation is for you to immediately take control of the situation by sending them forward and giving them something to think about. This will only be effective if that relationship has been developed on the ground. Once back on track, they will again be trying to please you, and you can respond with love and appreciation.

When Submissive horses are not being listened to, they internalize. The ones with Energy are the horses who crib and weave and have ulcers. But these Submissive ones, being Lazy, will show their stress in a more subtle way. They will glaze over and shut down, probably still trying to do the correct thing to avoid trouble with the look of one who no longer wants to interact or engage. It is sad to see this horse disconnected from his Friendly.

In the SLAF, the canter can be slow to be developed as they do not carry a lot of their own impulsion. They like to mentally take things in slowly so the canter can make them feel rushed or worried; pushing them to have more impulsion or revs can make them be worried that they are not doing the right thing. As with all their other training, allow it to develop slowly. If at first they can only carry it for four or five strides, reward them for that and they will keep building on it trying to please you. Positive repetition will carry you a long way on this horse. Take the time it takes. When the SLAF gets it—he has it! It will always be there. You can relax knowing that they are not trying to outsmart you or get away with something.

Careers

The SLAF wants easy tasks that do not require a lot of effort mentally or physically. They work for you and not the job. They can do a boring, menial task daily and as long as you are happy with them, they will be satisfied.

As older horses, they will become the solid school master. They can be good school horses in any discipline or be a low level competitive horse. A junior or child will be safe on them in their later years if they are solid in their training. And once they feel safe with their rider, they are wonderful pleasure horses because they want the relationship and love the loving. This is the horse that will meet you at the gate—just to be with you.

Chapter 20

SLAA   The Lone Wolf

Out on the hill, sitting by himself, howling at the moon is the lone wolf. Why is he not with the pack? Have they rejected him or has he rejected them? Why does he sing his own song? He intrigues us.

In your pasture there is a horse that is separate from the others, and we wonder as well, who has rejected whom? He is only social enough to keep safe. Even his herd instinct, you sense, he would like to deny some of the time. He appears not to care—about the herd and about us. We want his attention. What do we need to do to get it? The SLAA, the Lone Wolf, intrigues us.

We step into his life with love and attention and a plan. He rejects them all, except the carrots. We think he needs to be happier, so we try even harder to engage him. He responds with worry or boredom, depending on the degree of pressure we have put on him. The line seems very thin. If we talk loud enough to get his attention, he jumps to worried and we have to go into reassurance mode.

Out on the trail we will find the same scenario. He is ambling along, a little too slowly, a little too disinterested— if it was a person you might say preoccupied—when suddenly something catches his eye and his flight instinct kicks in. He nearly jumps out from underneath you. You find yourself just that little bit angry saying, "Wake up and pay attention, didn't you see it coming?" His world is crashing in on him; he now needs reassurance. We slightly resent that he now needs us. Why does he constantly flip between not paying attention and then overreacting?

Perhaps his personality traits can help us understand. He is Submissive, whether in the herd or with us. He seldom challenges. Most would describe him as soft and sweet, but difficult to get to know. He wants to be safe. To feel safe with us he probably needs a quiet hand and a reassuring leg. To this we add the Lazy trait, which is what makes him unexpressive and unemotional unless extremely afraid. The Lazy horse can get dull if we keep our leg on too much. To make our time together more enjoyable, we need to keep our workouts short and interesting. In schooling, do lots of transitions. His Afraid trait says that he wants routine and order. If he were a person you might find him in the research department. He will not take kindly or quietly to surprises. In training you might feel he is bored, so you add a bit of excitement with some new and interesting things to do. Rejected again! Bad idea! He doesn't mind bored. He appears to like it. His last trait, Aloof, means he is happy left alone, and also quite happy to work alone once we have engaged him. The Aloof needs a job, but he does not need an exciting job. Most of our recreational riding is sports-oriented, and most of these sports are too stressful for the SLAA. This may explain why a very small percentage of the horse population is this personality.

Surprisingly the Lone Wolf can have a very nurturing side. Lone Wolf mares are excellent mothers. This is the type of job they find rewarding. A way for a gelding to be nurturing is to be the caretaker or babysitter of a group of weanlings. Their quiet, solid, grounding influence will be very comforting for the babies. This personality would be a great companion horse for an orphan foal. A Lone Wolf I met in France used this nurturing ability to find a job she loved. She became a pony horse on the race track. She would take the youngsters to the starting gate or out to gallop. She settled right in to her job galloping quietly beside the high energy racer. Her calm nature helped the youngsters settle right down into their work. Her owner was thrilled that she had finally found something that made this mare happy.

In training this horse there will be no instant gratification. You will need to be there for the long haul. You will need to work quietly and slowly, with no expectations. You will need to be enough of a leader that they feel safe. You will need to find creative ways to motivate this individual without stressing him. He will want to withdraw. Trust can be broken easily. You must maintain a steadfast course. He will not likely reward you with ribbons and glory. Your reward will be the soft expression of happiness you see in his eye as he works at his tasks and knows that he has done a good job.

Training

Like the Wall Flower (SLAF), the Lone Wolf needs to be taught slowly and patiently as he can be easily misread. He will appear deceivingly quiet and accepting, tempting his trainer to push him beyond his ability and comfort level. Start with a solid foundation of ground work so that you have something to fall back on if a problem arises later on. This is not a horse that you can skip steps with. He is still afraid even though he does not outwardly show it. Honor his fear and allow him to learn things slowly. He is happy to repeat things often and will feel safer in that type of program.

Learning to appreciate what effort he gives is very important as he does not feel very accepted in the field or the arena. This is not the horse that thinks for himself.

Flatwork is mind settling to him. As he is Aloof, not Friendly, he will not demonstrate a great desire to please, therefore you must give him purpose in his work. Some type of small job that he enjoys early on will give him some motivation for the training. Finding that small job may not be easy. Most Aloofs are waiting to attack a project and get on with it, but not this Aloof. He appears happy to be left out of it all. Clicker training (see "Tools") would be a helpful tool to motivate him, but you must still be a strong leader as his main priority in life is to be kept safe.

This horse is happy to be ridden in contact because it keeps him safe. He likes to be told where to put every step. He is happy to be the master of a small job: a low key, low energy, low stress job. He does not need variety in his life. In fact, he would like to avoid variety. Change in jobs, owners or pastures are stressful for this personality. Same fare everyday is great with him. He is not looking for stimulation and excitement. If pushed into that type of environment, he can become explosive and fearful as it is too overwhelming for him to handle. If this horse does suddenly react, it always takes people by surprise as they are sure he is the "quiet good guy."

The type of rider best suited for a Lone Wolf is tricky to recommend because the dominant, strong rider will likely put on too much pressure and the submissive, quiet rider may not be enough of a leader to keep him safe. A person who can ride that fine line between the two would probably suit him best. All they would need to do is add love and patience. Perhaps a person who can take a matter of fact approach would be best suited to work with a Lone Wolf. If this horse has come into your life, you are probably being asked to become a leader, one who leads with quiet confidence and a well laid-out plan.

Careers

Just as the lone wolf sings his own song, this horse will have his own thing that he will be interested in. Your job as his owner is finding what that is, as it will be hard to motivate him to sing *your* song.

To the farmer a century ago, this personality would have been a real asset as a work horse. Perhaps we see few of them today because we primarily use horses for sports and that is not the ideal arena for the Lone Wolf. Following a furrow all day long might have really satisfied him, as he would have felt safe, had a partner that he could help, and a meaningful, predictable job. Our modern-day jobs are probably a bit too energetic, intense and emotionally demanding for this personality. Give him a solid day of work to do and time to himself to rest and relax and he just might be happy.

Perhaps the Lone Wolf is best suited as a pleasure horse if he can find the right owner. If ridden regularly, he might be happy on the trail, or working in the ring doing flatwork. He may compete in low level hunters, as he would enjoy the repetition of the courses if his rider is patient teaching it to him initially. In later years, at a job that he knew well, he could possibly be a good lesson horse, though he may always be too insecure to be a children's horse. If you have a job, that you think another horse might be bored at, this could be your horse.

Section III

Quick Reference

Chapter 21

Tools

The Round Pen

The round pen is your classroom of learning where the truth is spoken. This is where you can learn to understand your horse's language. The remarkable turn-around in some horses from a session in the round pen is because FINALLY they are being listened to. We are finally using their language instead of constantly insisting that they use ours. It is similar to when you are in a foreign country and you quit being self-conscious and start trying to speak their language. Chances are you will be met with smiles and enthusiasm. They will be anxious to please you and will remember you when they see you again.

Our horses will respond in the same way. When you step into the round pen and speak their language, horses will start to tell you what their emotional needs are, how friendly they are, how brave they are, how smart they are, how athletic they are, how confident they are, who they are. How you respond will tell the horse how much he can trust you, how much he wants to be with you, how much he wants to please you, or if he wants a relationship at all.

The main challenge for us from a body language point of view is that our ears are not expressive, and so we must learn to use our bodies to communicate. After walking an hour in the round pen with little results, we start to become more interested in body language. If you have ever observed your herd when you add a new horse, you will see how they speak this language and get tips on how to improve your pronunciation. You are in a foreign country: observe and learn the customs.

The best conversationalists are the best listeners. Nowhere is that more evident than in the round pen. There has been much written about the language of the round pen. But it is usually about our language and how we get the horse to listen to our requests. To understand the round pen process there are a couple of common concepts that are applicable. One is the "send," which is about pushing the horse away from you. The other is the "draw," which is about you becoming soft and appealing or non-threatening to the horse so that he comes towards you, wanting to be with you. They both start with energy and intent and then increase or decrease in activity until you are communicating.

To **"send"** you will need to get your energy up, chest up, stand tall, and look directly at your horse. To get forward movement you need to send from behind the shoulder of the horse. The soft high-energy horse will move off with a slight suggestion of your body or perhaps your arm. With the Lazy or Dominant horse you may need to up the pressure which could mean using a rope, a whip or your halter shank to swing at him to tell him to get moving. Each time you send, you want to start at the slightest suggestion. It may be a look, a sound, a point or a walk toward him. Then you gradually build the pressure until he moves off. Decide what order you will use and be consistent at it. At the slightest effort on his part, it is important that you stop advancing forward or increasing pressure. If he rushes off in a canter, you may have increased the pressure too quickly. Your goal is to be able to get him to walk off quietly and calmly. At that point you know you have fine-tuned your send to be just the right amount of pressure.

The **"draw"** is a way to ask your horse to come to you, a way to take all the pressure off and invite him in to be with you. As we do not have those fabulous ears that are so great at communicating when to go and when to come, we have to fumble along with our inept body language. For many of us, just to be aware that we have body language is a huge step. We need to make our bodies as soft and inviting as possible. Start by looking down, away from the horse, soften your shoulders, almost slump and then take the pressure off by backing away from your horse or even turning your body sideways. As your horse turns to come into you, keep backing away and allow him to follow you. When he has caught up to you, stop and spend time with him. For the very timid horse, he may not feel safe enough to follow initially. He may just turn and stop and look at you. If that is all you get at first, just stop and wait for him to be more comfortable. You could approach him quietly at that point. If he needs to move off, let him and begin quietly driving again. Next time you ask for the draw, he may be more comfortable and safe with you and start to take steps toward you.

If your horse is high-strung and revving to run when you turn him loose, let him. Sit in the middle and wait. This is an important way to prove to the horse that you do not have a big agenda. When he settles down and is walking or wanting to come in, then the games can begin. Plan to spend twenty minutes or a half hour in the round pen each day if he is a new horse that you want to get to know. Put aside any expectations of what you are going to accomplish in that half hour and see what happens when you approach him in that manner. If you have a friend that wants something from you every day that you see her, it isn't long until you are very guarded in that relationship or you decide the relationship is not worth it. See what trust can develop when your horse understands that you no longer need something from him.

Honoring your horse when he is with you is most important to build the trusting relationship that you want. Do not barge into his space, slapping and patting him. Wait for him to invite you to touch him. Just as you would not walk up and touch a stranger, wait until you have spent some time together before you begin touching. Even allow your horse to initiate the process. Allow him to touch you first, then only pet him once for every time he touches you. This is the start of dialogue. You can even do that before you start the round pen session. It will tell your horse right away that he is going to be listened to.

My observations have been that in the herd, horses do not run the new horse for long periods of time—that would require too much work on their part and they do not have the round pen as a tool! The round pen is typically designed so we can work horses hard with little effort on our part, which is, when you think about it, a bit of an unfair advantage. The horse in this situation and with this direct approach may finally come in because he realizes the futility of running away from us, but have we really built trust and the foundation for the type of relationship that we want?

Again, in observing the herd, horses push the new horse away and then they go back to the herd to wait, eat and just be. Sometimes this is done at a run, but frequently it is just at a walk. They are quietly saying, "Go away, you are not part of our herd yet." We have problems in our trainer minds and our trainer time to wait and be. We want to control every step. We want to hurry the process. Trainers even set times saying they can always get "Join Up" (when the horse wants to come in and follow you as the leader) in thirty minutes. But as we wait and be and allow the horse to process and come in on his terms, he starts to see us in a new light. We have truly stepped out of that predator role. We are now a leader that he feels safe to interact with, safe to play with, safe to bond and do mutual grooming with. Horse leadership is not just about control and domination, and I believe most people want much more out of their interaction with the horse as well.

Many trainers use the round pen to start young horses, but the value for the owner with the sixteen year-old is just as great. The round pen is a tool you can use to connect with your horse on a new level and a place to learn to play. Suddenly it is not all about work. He will want to be on your page because you are trying to learn his language. You will understand better how he naturally processes new information. This will change how you train. You will see who your horse truly is, and he will see your truth. The round pen always speaks the truth.

Each horse is an individual and in the freedom of the round pen we begin to see that. There are sixteen personalities that all want to be treated differently, but within each of these, we have the opportunity to see the individual traits. The Dominant horses will come in sassy wanting to challenge you and change direction and call the shots. When you send them out, they kick at you and tell you how they feel. Don't take it personally—they are used to controlling their world. Gradually they will come around to being with you on your level, and you will not have snuffed their enthusiasm and expression. In most sports and situations we admire these qualities.

The Submissive horse's reaction in the round pen will vary from soft and sticky to running away from you. The soft sticky type that want to only be with you (like the People Pleasers or the Wall Flowers) will gradually gain confidence to be out on his own. He learns that when you send him away he is not being shunned, that you still love him and will bring him in again soon. The Submissives with a lot of energy, or those who are extremely fearful, may be hard to draw in and so your patience and your ability to BE may be severely tested. But be aware that working this horse harder will only increase the chasm between you. This sometimes flighty, impulsive, reactive horse will eventually settle and start to trust not only you but his world. He will not have to be so "on guard." The quiet fearful horse will finally quit internalizing everything and realize that he can express himself because he will be listened to. As he begins to express himself, he will quit being unpredictable and stuck.

If your horse is secure and confident, this time spent with him in the round pen will be play time that cements your bond. If he has emotional issues, this is your therapeutic couch. If he has physical issues, this can be a soft, non-stressful time where he can start to heal by releasing old emotional problems. If the horse is new to you, this is a great starting place to establish new working ground rules. Round pen work enables you to spend some quality time with young horses and to establish boundaries. You will also be able to figure out their personalities with a session or two in the round pen.

It's not about the pen—you do not need to go and buy a fancy prefab round pen made to a prescribed dimension and height. It does not even have to be round. A square paddock with good footing is fine. An end of your arena temporarily fenced off will do. All that is required is a space and place where you and your horse can play.

Clicker Training

There are books, tapes and clinics on clicker training if you want to truly understand the philosophy as well as all the applications for it. Here I will present a small introduction and a few tips on using this positive reward system, although I am by no means a clinician or teacher on clicker training. I have used it and seen it used with very positive results. For some of the more difficult personalities, I feel it is almost a must, especially if they are already working a negative aspect of their personality.

Clicker training is not bribing your horse to do something for you. It is rewarding or marking a behavior that you want to be repeated. For some of the Dominant and Aloof horses it is giving them a reason to want to please you. For some of the Energy and Afraid horses it is motivating them to stay in the thinking part of their brains rather than slipping into a reactive mode. If you are feeling stuck with a problem, you may want to reach for this tool and give it a try.

Clicker training is a great tool for children to use. They love the positive aspect of it. They understand how much better it is to be rewarded rather than reprimanded. It allows children to teach their ponies, which is a very empowering thing for them. They should not have the use of negative training methods such as spurs or whips. Clicker training gives them a way to make changes in behavior. For some ponies that are the classic "cookie monsters," this tool might be best used only during riding so that they are not pushy with the children when they are on the ground. One of the main benefits for children is that they begin to look for the positive things their ponies are doing rather than feeling frustrated because the pony is doing "bad" things.

In the beginning, you want to establish a link between a sound and a reward, because in riding we want to make a sound at exactly the moment the horse does the desired behavior. Some clicker trainers use a clicker device. I use a "cluck" sound with the front of my tongue because it is always available. It is important to differentiate the cluck from the "click/click" that many riders use to get their horses to go forward. Simply put, the horse learns that the cluck is followed by a treat reward. Once he knows that, then the cluck sound can be made at exactly the moment the horse does a desired behavior (followed by a treat). Some clicker trainers reward every time they cluck while others do it randomly.

To start, you want to teach your horse that he must not touch you or "mug" you to get treats. The desired behavior is for the horse to turn his head away from you when you hold out a treat. You offer it to him, but he must never take it. To do this, stand on one side by your horse's shoulder and hold a treat in your hand. The horse will begin sniffing and trying to get at the treat. When he finally gives up and goes to move his head away, cluck and immediately give him the treat. At first, the move may only be an inch or two. Gradually raise the bar so that he has to move his head further before you cluck/treat. He will soon begin to move his head away from you when you approach, rather than touching and poking you for cookies. As soon as he has the one side, repeat the process on the other side. It is important that the treat is ready and that you give it to him very close to the time you clucked and when his head is away from you. You have created a conditioned response that you will then build on and use in many different situations.

You can now use this sound/reward (cluck/treat) to play with your horse and teach him tricks or to use it to re-school certain behaviors. Some tricks might be touching something with their nose, picking up something in their mouths, kicking a ball with their front feet, standing on a block, jumping over an object—the list is as long as your imagination. It allows you to put fun back into the time you spend together.

For the training part of it, we will take a behavior like not standing for mounting, and see how to use it. If the minute you gather up your reins and move toward the saddle, your horse is on the move you will need to step back and find the first thing that triggered his reaction. Break it down into baby steps. If you can do step one and he stands, then cluck/treat. Step one might be just moving into the shoulder position without gathering up the reins. Then gradually build on that, can he stand while you pick up the reins? Can he stand while you lift one foot? Can you get part way up and then down again? Keep moving the reward to the next little step. When you are on him, it will not take him long to figure out how to bring his nose around to your foot and get a treat (cookies work best for this). Standing to be mounted is such an important safety issue, that it is worth the time it takes the first time. Once established, it will always be there.

In riding, clicker training can be used to teach or correct specific movements such as the canter or the stop. Break it down the same way as mounting. If you are having trouble getting the canter, when you cue and he picks it up, cluck. He will break to the walk and probably stop to get his cookie. This is fine. Build on it so that he does a few strides at the canter before you cluck. Eventually, he will be cantering circles. For the stop, cue the "whoa" and with any recognition or attempt by the horse to slow or stop, cluck and treat. This will come very quickly. To build on it, ask for the stop and then one step backwards before the cluck/treat. You will need to always stay one step ahead using this tool.

Having problems bridling? Break it down and cluck/treat each step until you have built up a worry and fight-free bridling experience. The same approach can be used for saddling.

Most movements in training will be improved once you improve the horses' impulsion. Most horses are either reluctant to go forward or reluctant to stop (Energy or Lazy). By using the clicker training to deal with this basic issue most other issues will be solved. If your horse is the Lazy type, try using it to reward just the forward for awhile. Once he understands forward, all other movements will be better. Conversely, the horse that is hot and hard to slow down needs help seeing that slowing down is the positive thing to do. They will usually be resistant to any hand pressure. If the only time they are getting a reward is when you take up the contact and ask for a downward transition, they soon start to look forward to the hand instead of resenting it. If forward or slowing down is still a problem after implementing clicker training to help fix it, you may need to check them out physically. They may be hurting, and the reaction is pain induced. Even clicker will not override it. In this situation, you will need to call your vet or chiropractor.

Keep it fun and keep it fresh. Not only does clicker help the horse have a more positive attitude, but it really helps us as riders to be constantly watching out for the positive behavior rather than disciplining for a negative one.

Dominant Leading

Most of the really valuable training tools have come to me from the horse. I was watching our herd heading out into a new field that we had opened up. The gate was narrow, about 6 feet. Our herd boss, whose name is Tony—which is short for Tony Soprano because he is short, fat and not one to be messed with—was taking his time heading out into the new grass. He stopped in the gate cautiously surveying the territory. The herd behind was anxious to get to the new grass, but did they do any head butting or pushing or pawing or show any signs of impatience? No. They stood quietly behind him waiting. They were not emotional in any way. They were waiting, with perfect respect. I watched this many mornings. It wasn't always Tony, but at any time someone higher in the pecking order stopped in the gate, those behind waited patiently. I realized that I wanted that kind of quiet respect from my horses.

I began to notice more and more the horses' order as they walked to and from different fields, usually in pecking order, almost always one behind the other unless they were running. The question arose: why do we get our horses to walk beside us when naturally they want to walk either in front or behind, like most other things in their lives, very dictated by pecking order? I realized that all my past training in how to lead horses, especially the thoroughbreds at the track, had been wrong. We would walk by their left shoulders, bending their heads into us, keeping an eye on them at all times. I think we were taught to lead that way so that we could always see what the horses were going to do. If they were behind you, they might bite or rear and you could be in danger. I wanted to let go of that fear and to teach them that behind was a safe respectful place to be.

I wouldn't walk in front of them until I could trust them. I needed to be able to see them and be in front. So step one was walking backward leading them. I carried a stick with me so that I could raise it and get the horse's attention if he went to push over me. It also allowed me to reach out to the side if he decided to speed up and try to go around me. I used it as a block not a weapon. I would walk and stop repeatedly until they could stay with me and stop and stand quietly when I did. When I asked for the stop, I would raise my rope and stick at first; then when the horse stopped, I would lower both and stand relaxed. Soon the horse was watching for the slightest hand movement. We were ready for step two.

Step two was to turn and walk facing forward and see if he could still stay behind rather than coming up beside me. At first when I stopped, I would raise my rope and turn and step in front of him, facing him. I would say whoa, raise the rope, then step in front of him. This created a good bridge from the walking backward exercise. I would do this exercise from both sides. I noticed the hardest side for most horses was the left because they have largely been programmed to be up beside their handler. Soon all I needed to do was raise my hand as we walked and the horse would stop. I no longer had to turn and make a big production out of the stop. They would wait patiently until I initiated the walk off. I had the respect I had been looking for on the ground in our arena.

Step three was making this exercise more interesting and testing it by increasing the challenge. Walking away from home is quite easy, walking back toward the barn or herd is more difficult. Sometimes as the bar is raised and the exercise is tougher, I needed to go back to leading backward. Using this progression, I have been able to build that quiet respect that I observed among the horses.

When working on dominant leading, work in a safe place to start, then add excitement gradually until the horse can maintain better emotional control. This exercise will not only make your horse a pleasure to be with on the ground but will also make him a more stable riding companion as he will have learned to trust you as a leader, and you have learned to move into new territory only when he is comfortable and ready.

Alternative method:

In doing workshops and teaching small children, I soon realized that they were not able to make themselves BIG enough for this exercise to be successful. I had them achieve the same result through a different technique, one that was easy to do. It was an experiment that worked for children and then got expanded into the whole program. I use it myself if a horse is a nervous, timid type, or if they are already fearful and untrusting of humans. The pushy spoiled type of horse needs the "get big, stick in the face, pay attention" type of method, while the scared horse that you are trying to up build trust with needs a softer method.

For this technique no stick is required, just a long lead line (approximately ten feet). Walk off and if—and when— your horse starts to go by you, abruptly turn and go the other direction. The horse will be surprised by the quick tug on the rope, and he will find himself behind you again. Soon he will probably overtake you again. Repeat this exercise again and again until he finds it is much easier to stay behind you and wait for a lead.

The stop will be done the same. Wait until you have led them for 10 or 15 minutes so that they are ready to stop. Say whoa, raise your rope and step in front of your horse facing him. Then drop your hands, stand and wait. Go into him and praise and reward him. Gradually build the time that he can stand and wait. For the high energy horse this will not be long. Build on the patience slowly. If possible, anticipate when he is about to move and beat him to it by going back to your leading exercise.

The horse will develop the same quiet accepting attitude after a few of these turns when he keeps finding himself yet again behind you. A bit of psychology or trickery, but either way he comes to the same conclusion: "if you are always in front, you must be the boss and therefore I am safe because I am in my place."

Use the same building blocks with this technique. Start in your arena or a safe place and then venture out into the yard or fields as your confidence in each other builds.

Once your horse has started to see you as the leader, it is important for you not to give up that respect in other areas. Be careful that you do not allow him to step into your space and make you give up yours. That is how horses dominate each other at the feed tub, and it is the way he will try to dominate you. If he steps into you and you get out of his way, he will try this again in other ways. You will have to start at the beginning again in your dominant leading exercise, as that one step backward has just told him that you really are not above him in the pecking order. This does not mean that you have to be a brute and keep beating your horse back, but it does mean that you have to be aware of subtle body language. How well you learn to use his language is how well he will treat you.

Chapter 22

Do's and Don't's for Each Personality

DECF   **The Rock Star**

Rock Stars are confident and charismatic. They are expressive and strong minded. They love to show you what they know but are hard to get to focus on the small details of the task. They are found in many competitive arenas, usually at the top of their field.

DO

Pamper their ego

Allow them to shine

Allow them to teach you

Allow them to think

Work them regularly

Treat them with dignity

Pet them/Love them

Respect them

DON'T

Coddle them

Pick at them

Be a perfectionist

Bore them

Be a taskmaster

DECA   The Macho Man

If you have a serious job to do, this is the horse for it. You will have to get out of the way and allow them some freedom in how they do it. Sit down, shut up and hold on! It is initially hard to get them to accept that you do know what you are talking about, so training in the beginning can be challenging. Use psychology and variety and start them into their career at a very early age.

DO

Honor them

Give them a job

Treat them with respect

Give them variety

Ride them a lot

DON'T

Fight with them

Be a taskmaster

Fuss over them

Bore them

"Pick" at them

DEAF   The Wild Card

Strong minded but insecure, this personality needs an equally strong rider to help them feel safe. Be loving and affectionate, but don't give up your leadership. Once you have them on your page, they are very friendly and have a strong desire to please. They can be highly competitive and will give you their all. Not a horse for a junior or amateur until much later in life.

DO
Protect them
Repeat lessons often
Be their boss
Honor their energy
Keep a steady training program

DON'T
Overload them
Skip steps in training
Show weakness or fear
Have huge expectations
Jump into new territory

DEAA   The Boss

This strong authority figure is all business and can be resistant and difficult if not working at a job that they like. They are usually the herd boss and are used to calling the shots and running the show. You will have this to overcome in training, and you will have to be there to help them get their job done as fear can easily overcome them. This horse will call on you to be firm, fair and fearless.

DO
Find them a job
Show them respect
Show them leadership
Work in the box
Build a solid foundation
DON'T
Skip training steps
Pamper and fuss over them
Be emotional
Fight with them
Play with them

DLCF   The Reluctant Rock Star

This horse has a big ego, loves attention, loves to be in the limelight, but doesn't really like all the work it takes to be there. That is where you come in. You will need to push, persuade and motivate every inch of the way.

DO
Help them to be a star
Keep work fun and exciting
Pamper their ego
Be firm about forward
Be affectionate
Go new places

DON'T
Drill them
Bore them with details
Nag them
Overwork them
Be all business
Under-value them

DLCA   The Prize Fighter

This horse has opinions and is ready to defend them. It is in your best interest to listen to him. To get the job done you must work with him. He will have numerous rules and requirements. He will also get you to the winner's circle when you have developed a working relationship. Unlike the Rock Star who is there for the glory and recognition, the Prize Fighter is there because they love the sport and the competition.

DO

Engage them in a job

Encourage forward

Keep workouts short and fun

Give them their space

Allow them their idiosyncrasies

Use positive motivation

DON'T

Make them see it your way

"Pick" at them

Bore them

Pet and pamper them

Put them in a box

Fight with them

DLAF   The Accountant

Slow, steady and determined describes this personality. They do not need excitement or fanfare. They like predictability. They want you to have a plan and stick to it. The friendship is important to them, so it is important for them to be honored and appreciated.

DO
Keep training progressive
Ride in the box
Repeat lessons often
Respect them
Be their friend and leader
Lots of positive reward

DON'T
Skip steps
Change routines
Surprise them
Be in a hurry
Have huge expectations
Bully them

DLAA   The Skeptic

To be happy this horse needs to be doing a small, quiet, repetitive job that may seem boring and unexciting to other personalities. They do not need or want a lot of attention or accolades. Just leave them to their simple tasks. If anything goes wrong, the Skeptic will look for someone to blame, and chances are, it will be you.

DO
Be a quiet, fair leader
Show them respect
Build trust slowly
Use positive reward
DON'T
Push them into new things
Fuss over them
Change the program
Fight with them

SECF   The Goddess

The Goddess is loved by most of the other horses and most people. They are expressive and sensitive and emotional. You will know how they feel. They try very hard to please and will worry and be anxious if you are not happy with them. In the negative they can have scattered energy that is hard to get focused.

DO

Listen to them

Play with them

Ask for what you want

Allow them friendships

Honor their horse friendships

Be their friend and leader

Give them variety

Own them forever

DON'T

Be rigid

Be bossy

Be boring

Move them frequently

Keep them alone

Stress them

SECA   The Worker Bee

It is all about the job for this horse. Hopefully they find one that they love, as then they can be that steady, consistent campaigner that everyone wants. In the beginning they may have trouble focusing and learning their trade. Once they learn it, they will perform it the same for every subsequent owner. They bore easily and like variety in their work. This is a great working horse, but he will likely have too much energy to be the weekend pleasure mount.

DO

Honor them emotionally

Keep them busy

Give them a variety of work

Give their work purpose

Be their leader

Show them how to do it

Have a well planned program

DON'T

Pamper them

Be indecisive

Bore them

Nitpick

Be grey and uncertain

Expect them to work solo

SEAF   The People Pleaser

Soft, sensitive, and very sweet describes this horse that will try and try to please you. They like to be told exactly what you want and then have you help them perform it. This is not your go-it-alone type of horse. They need you for support and can get very rattled if expectations are too high. This horse is in your life for the relationship.

DO

Be a calm and quiet leader

Slow things down until they get it

Love them—honor their Friendly

Reassure constantly

Build a solid foundation

DON'T

Overface them (set a fence too high)

Skip steps in training

Be loud or crude

Use negative reinforcement

SEAA   The Perfectionist

Shy, suspicious, sensitive! Are you a solid, consistent enough rider with low enough expectations to be able to work with this horse? They need a solid, well planned out training program to be able to perform well. They want a job that they can perform perfectly. Each step in the training process needs to be methodical and repeated until they really, really get it. If things get too hard to handle, this horse's evasion is simply to leave—mentally, emotionally, and physically if possible. If they find a job they like and are allowed to learn it slowly and correctly, they will give you an endless amount of effort.

DO
Be a firm fair leader
Allow a lot of exercise
Keep them in a safety box
Use baby steps/safety circles
Provide solid guidelines

DON'T
Be wishy-washy
Fuss over them
Change the program
Skip steps in training
Speed up until solid

SLCF   The Steady Eddy

If you are a novice or amateur, this is the horse for you. They are quiet and predictable, loving and engaging, willing to learn new things, willing to hang out with you and do nothing. This is not your big ego, career-oriented horse. They are happy to just be. Consistent and loyal, all you need to do is enjoy!

DO
Whatever you want
Appreciate them
Play with them
Keep variety in their work
Keep workouts short

DON'T
Have huge expectations
Overtax them
Ignore them
Bore them

SLCA   The Solo Artist

This horse needs a job, but not just any job, certainly not one that you chose for him, but a job that he wants to do. He is not easily motivated, so forcing him to do the job of your choice is going to be a long and arduous task. Although not overly enthused, this horse is still a quiet, good mount for most riders. If you can find the job he likes, it will get done with enthusiasm and efficiency.

DO
Be creative
Find a job they like
Short, quick workouts
Lots of variety
DON'T
Get locked into a set way
Be a taskmaster
Fight with them
Take it personally

SLAF   The Wall Flower

Wrap these sweet, kind, gentle horses up and keep them safe. They are not very brave and tend to internalize their worries. They want to please and will try very hard for you, but they can be pushed too fast very easily. They make few demands of you and are quite content to perform the same tasks repeatedly as long as you are pleased with them and the jobs are not too strenuous. They can be quiet enough for the beginner once they understand what is expected of them.

DO
Be their leader
Keep them safe
Build trust slowly
Keep tasks simple & repetitive
Cuddle them lots
Spend the time it takes
Appreciate them
DON'T
Expect them to go solo
Scare them
Overface them (set a fence too high)
Be overly demanding
Ignore them
Hurry them
Take them for granted

SLAA   The Lone Wolf

Low key, low energy, low expectations, are what you need to work successfully with this type of horse. The Lone Wolf is not bursting out of his stall to try to fit into your program and to please you. He is easily content and can do a good job for you as long as it is not demanding physically or emotionally. He likes his world predictable and safe. He would rather be a little bored than stressed. If repeatedly put into pressure situations he can react unpredictably. If you can find a quiet solid job for him, he will perform it repeatedly and safely.

DO

Be a quiet leader

Keep them safe

Appreciate what effort they give

Repeat it until they are solid

Stay the course

Venture out slowly

Find them an easy, low stress job

DON'T

Abandon them

Scare them

Compare them to others

Skip steps

Jump from job to job

Assume they can handle it

Chapter 23

The Personality Quiz

One way to find out what your horse's personality is to read the descriptions in Section I to see if you can identify your horse's traits. Put a check mark next to the one in each pair you think describes your horse. Put them together into a personality. For example, if you check off Dominant, Lazy, Curious, Aloof, you have a Prize Fighter.

My horse:
Dominant _____ **or** Submissive _____?
Energetic _____ **or** Lazy _____?
Curious _____ **or** Afraid _____?
Friendly _____ **or** Aloof _____?

Some horses are puzzling especially if they are near the dividing line between two different traits (for example, Energetic and Lazy). In general, these middle horses are usually the easiest to work with as they are usually flexible and a more balanced individual.

In any pair of traits, if your horse is very easy to categorize—I call it "off the chart"—put a star beside that trait because it will affect the other traits in his personality. For example, any horse who is extremely Energetic, the E is going to make the other characteristics seem stronger. He will put more energy into his dominance—the fight can last longer. He will put more energy into his fear—he will run further. He will put more energy into his Aloof—just try and catch me. Extremely Lazy is going to challenge you to find ways to motivate him. With the horse that is extremely Afraid everything is going to take longer, and you will always need to be aware of that trait or the horse can derail even though his other attributes are very positive. Extremely Curious says keep me engaged or I will find ways to entertain myself (might not always be positive). You would not think that extremely Friendly is a negative attribute, but these horses do need your constant approval and attention. We run into trouble with their insecurity about being alone. Aloof in the extreme—now that can be a huge problem but only if you have not given that horse a job. In fact, this horse demands a job or you may not see him or at any rate catch him.

A horse with three or four starred traits is way out there. In the positive, they are top of their field. In the negative, you need a psychology degree to deal with them.

The Personality Quiz

You may want to use the Personality Quiz below to help you figure out your horse's personality. Bear in mind that this is not scientific but may more easily identify your horse's traits and thus his personality. Here's how it works. Read each question and then assign a score:

0 = never or unsure
1 = sometimes
2 = usually
3 = always

1. At feed time, does your horse eat in the top half of the herd's pecking order? Score: _____
2. Is your horse easy to get to go forward? Score: _____

3.   Is your horse interested in investigating new objects? Score: _____

4.   Does your horse like to be touched, petted and groomed? Score: _____

5.   Does your horse wait to eat and drink in the bottom half of the pecking order? Score: _____

6.   Is your horse dull to your leg? Score: _____

7.   Does your horse look to you to keep him safe? Score: _____

8.   Does your horse frequently graze separately from the herd? Score: _____

9.   If you reprimand your horse when working him, is he likely to kick out or respond with a buck? Score: _____

10.   Does your horse settle and have more focus after a twenty-minute loose rein warm-up? Score: _____

11.   Does your horse like to play with gates, latches, or chains? Score: _____

12.   Will your horse leave the herd to approach you? Score: _____

13.   Does your horse like you to be there for him every step of the way? Score: _____

14.   Is your horse happy and content to stand still? Score: _____

15.   Is your horse happy to do the same job over and over again? Score: _____

16.   Is your horse sometimes hard to catch? Score: _____

17.   When leading your horse and you stop, is he likely to push you to get going or try to barge past you? Score: _____

18. On the trail, does your horse want to push by to get into the lead? Score: _____
19. Does your horse like to go new places? Score: ___
20. Is your horse bonded strongly to other herd members and sometimes whinnies and screams when separated from them? Score: _____
21. Is your horse content to be controlled? Score: __
22. On the trail is your horse content to be last? Score: _____
23. Is your horse worried going into new environments? Score: _____
24. Does your horse need to have a purpose? Score: _____
25. When performing in his sport, does your horse need to have some say in how he does his job? Score: _____
26. Is your horse sensitive and light to the leg? Score: _____
27. Does your horse get bored easily if asked to do the same exercise over and over again? Score: _____
28. Is your horse well-liked by other herd members? Score: _____
29. If you reprimand your horse, is he more likely to become afraid than angry? Score: _____
30. Would you describe your horse as quiet? Score: _____
31. Does your horse prefer others to lead in a new situation? Score: _____
32. Does your horse avoid contact with strangers? Score: _____
33. Does your horse challenge your authority? Score: _____

34. Is your leg more likely to mean forward than sideways? Score: _____
35. Does your horse like playing games with others in the herd or with you? Score: _____
36. Does your horse have a strong desire to please? Score: _____
37. Does your horse get worried if he is not sure what you want him to do? Score: _____
38. Does your horse prefer "whoa" to "go"? Score: _____
39. Does your horse require a long time to establish trust? Score: _____
40. Does your horse have a strong work ethic? Score: _____
41. Does your horse demand a lot of attention? Score: _____
42. Is your horse impatient when asked to stand still? Score: _____
43. When learning a new sport, is your horse more interested and excited than wary or worried? Score: _____
44. Will your horse approach and touch people he does not know? Score: _____
45. Is your horse a "bully" when he is in a position of authority? Score: _____
46. If your horse is upset, is he more likely to buck than run off? Score: _____
47. Does your horse remain suspicious and wary of new things for a long time? Score: _____
48. Does your horse handle being alone better than most horses? Score: _____
49. Are upward transitions easier than downward transitions? Score: _____

50. Does your horse seem to tire easily? Score: _____
51. Does your horse get upset if you change the program? Score: _____
52. Would you describe your horse as busy and expressive? Score: _____
53. Does your horse like a lot of variety in his work? Score: _____
54. Does your horse prefer to move laterally rather than forward? Score: _____

Dominant (D) or Submissive (S)?

Add the scores for questions 1, 9, 17, 25, 33, and 41. _____ = D
Then add the scores for questions 5, 13, 21, 29, 37, and 45. _____ = S
My horse is (choose the highest between D and S) _____.

Energetic (E) or Lazy (L)?

Add the scores for questions 2, 10, 18, 26, 34, 42, 49, and 52. _____= E
Then add the scores for questions 6, 14, 22, 30, 38, 46, 50, and 54. _____= L
My horse is (choose the highest between E and L) _____.

Curious (C) or Afraid (A):

Add the scores for questions 3, 11, 19, 27, 35, 43, and 53. _____= C
Then add the scores for questions 7, 15, 23, 31, 39, 47, and 51. _____= A
My horse is (choose the highest between C and A) _____.

Friendly (F) or Aloof (A)?
Add the scores for questions 4, 12, 20, 28, 36,
and 44. _____ = F
Then add the scores for questions 8, 16, 24, 32, 40,
and 48 _____ = A
My horse is (choose the highest between F
and A) _____.

Altogether, the four letters of my horse's
personality are: _____.

My horse is a: _____

Refer back to Section II for a description of the
personality as revealed by the Personality Quiz. Does
this make sense to you? Now, go have some fun with your
fabulous equine friend!

2735472

Made in the USA